Journal of Educ
Psychological C

Volume 14, Num

T0314621

*Special Issue Action Editors: Emilia C. Lopez and Kathleen C. Harris

First published 2003 by Lawrence Erlbaum Associates, Inc.

This edition published 2013 by Routledge

711 Third Avenue, New York, NY 10017
2 Park Square, Milton Park, Abingdon, Oxon OX14 4RN

*Routledge is an imprint of the Taylor & Francis Group,
an informa business*

JOURNAL OF EDUCATIONAL AND PSYCHOLOGICAL CONSULTATION, 14(3&4), 241
Copyright © 2003, Lawrence Erlbaum Associates, Inc.

EDITOR'S NOTE

Acknowledgments

Manuscripts submitted to the *Journal of Educational and Psychological Consultation* (*JEPC*) are reviewed by our Editorial Review Board members. The following colleagues served as ad hoc reviewers for manuscripts submitted in 2003.

Jeff Braden
Mary Alice Heuschel
Patricia S. Lynch
Margaret J. McLaughlin
Ann Nevin
Judith A. Niemeyer

The *JEPC* editorial staff would like to thank the members of the Editorial Review Board and the ad hoc reviewers for their feedback, expertise, and support.

Emilia C. Lopez
Editor

Article of the Year Award

The *Journal of Educational and Psychological Consultation* (*JEPC*) will present an annual Article of the Year Award. The award will be granted to the author(s) of an article published in *JEPC* during 2004 (Volume 15, Issues 1–4). Articles will be nominated and rated for the award by members of the Editorial Review Board. The article rated highest in terms of its contribution to research and practice in consultation will receive the award. The author(s) will receive an Article of the Year Award certificate and a $200 check.

Correspondence should be addressed to Emilia C. Lopez, Queens College-CUNY, Educational and Community Programs, 65-30 Kissena Blvd., Flushing, NY 11367. E-mail: lopez@cedx.com

JOURNAL OF EDUCATIONAL AND PSYCHOLOGICAL CONSULTATION, 14(3&4), 243–250

SPECIAL ISSUE
INTRODUCTION

Current Research in
Consultee-Centered Consultation

Steven E. Knotek

University of North Carolina, Chapel Hill

Jonathan Sandoval

University of California, Davis

Gerald Caplan's (1970) classic text, *The Theory and Practice of Mental Health Consultation*, was first issued more than 30 years ago. In it, he outlined the use of consultation as an indirect means to promote mental health in clients through the practice of four basic forms of consultation to professionals. Of the four varieties of mental health consultation that he outlined in the text, one variety, consultee-centered consultation, has received considerable attention and has been the most closely associated with Caplan (Brown, Pryzwansky, & Schulte, 2001). Since the appearance of the text, psychologists and mental health professionals in the United States and other countries have adapted the method to a wide variety of settings with professionals in many work roles. Over the past 30 years notions about the method have evolved as Caplan's original formulations have been tried and modified based on experience and successful practice. In countries such as Sweden, but also in the United States, practitioners have elevated consultee-centered consultation to the forefront of approaches for helping other professionals, such as teachers, be more effective in working with cli-

Correspondence should be addressed to Steven E. Knotek, CB#3500, 103 Peabody, School of Education, University of North Carolina at Chapel Hill, Chapel Hill, NC 27514-3500. E-mail: sknotek@email.unc.edu

ents. As consultee-centered consultation has been adopted and changed to suit the needs of consultants in diverse contexts, it has evolved beyond the original definition and boundaries of mental health consultation that were first presented by Caplan.

Through the decades consultants have used and modified classic consultee-centered consultation such that a gap has emerged between the published and generally accepted understanding of its contemporary practice. Even though Caplan himself published a revised edition of the text in 1993, and reconfigured some aspects of the model (Caplan & Caplan, 1993), many practitioners still identify consultee-centered consultation with its 1970 definition and with such concepts as a psychodynamic orientation and the issue of theme interference. Those who had been both adapting the practice of consultee-centered consultation and training consultants to use the method, such as Nadine Lambert at the University of California and Gunilla Guvå at Linkoping University in Sweden, have found that the generally understood conception of the method, particularly the linkage of mental health with psychodynamic theory, were not reflective of its current use (Lambert, Hylander, & Sandoval, 2003). The practice of consultee-centered consultation had outstripped the recognized orthodoxy.

To address the incongruency between the perceived canon and the actual practice, three international seminars have been held wherein consultants and trainers have met and discussed their current understandings of consultee-centered consultation. Between 1996 and 2001, two international seminars were held in Stockholm, Sweden, and one in San Francisco, California. This special issue will present some of the outcomes of those seminars.

In this introduction, the current and older conceptions of consultee-centered consultation are compared. Next, consultee-centered consultation is compared to another widely used form of consultation, namely behavioral consultation. Finally, the articles that follow the introduction will be described.

CONSULTEE-CENTERED CONSULTATION RECONSIDERED

Considerable time was spent at the international seminars presenting examples of the participants' use of consultee-centered consultation and in collaborating on a new definition. The contemporary definition of *consultee-centered consultation* developed at these seminars is as follows:

1. Consultee-centered consultation emphasizes a non-hierarchical helping role relationship between a resource (consultant) and a person or group (consultee) who seeks professional help with a work problem involving a third party (client).

2. This work problem is a topic of concern for the consultee who has a direct responsibility for the learning, development, or productivity of the client.

3. The primary task of the consultant is to help the consultee pinpoint critical information and then consider multiple views about well-being, development, intrapersonal, interpersonal, and organizational effectiveness appropriate to the consultee's work setting. Ultimately, the consultee may reframe his or her prior conceptualization of the work problem.

4. The goal of the consultation process is the joint development of a new way of conceptualizing the work problem so that the repertoire of the consultee is expanded and the professional relationship between the consultee and the client is restored or improved. As the problem is jointly reconsidered, new ways of approaching the problem may lead to acquiring new means to address the work dilemma.

CORE ISSUES IN THE DEVELOPMENT OF A NEW DEFINITION

The new definition has evolved from the original model in three important ways (see Table 1). First, the current model uses a constructivist perspective in which conceptual change becomes the intrapsychic goal of the consultation process, which is in contrast to the original psychodynamic formulation (Sandoval, this issue). Conceptual change in the consultant and the consultee are hallmarks of the process.

TABLE 1
Differences Between Mental Health Consultation and Consultee-Centered Consultation

Dimension	Mental Health Consultation	Consultee-Centered Consultation
Organizing theory	Psychodynamic	Constructivist
Stance in organization	External, no responsibility for case	Internal or external, may have responsibility for the case
Settings	Primarily focus mental health (e.g., clinics)	Schools, day care centers, and clinics

Second, this model has a different perspective on the issue of consultants being internal to the organization, and in a related vein, on the difference between consultation and collaboration. Caplan & Caplan (1993) maintained that the consultant must be external to the organization and not responsible for the delivery of any direct services to the client. However, as mental health consultation evolved and as consultee-centered consultation was developed, the application of consultation has spread from traditional mental health settings to include schools and daycare institutions. In the current conceptualization and practice of consultee-centered consultation, the consultant is often a member of the organization and may be required to provide direct service. Working within a human service organization implies that all members have some responsibility to serve the clients. In the many settings in which consultee-centered consultation is currently practiced, service roles may be differentiated with varying levels of responsibility in a domain assigned to an individual professional. Associated with the practice of consultation by an internal professional is a related issue as to when a consultant ceases to consult and instead begins to collaborate.

The issue of consultation versus collaboration is not unique to the specialty of consultee-centered consultation and has been discussed in the general consultation literature (Pryzwansky, 1977; Schulte & Osborne, 1993; West & Idol, 1993). The distinction between consultation and collaboration is often made around an either–or statement about whether or not the professional is providing direct or indirect help (Brown et al., 2001). However, in some of the settings in which consultee-centered consultation is practiced consultants find themselves in a both–and situation. They are in the role of both using consultation to support the client indirectly by fostering the intellectual, contextual (i.e., responsive to social and ethnic factors), and emotional growth of consultees; also, if their professional role dictates it, they may be directly involved in the problem-solving process as a collaborator on a particular case.

This dichotomous role is especially prevalent in school settings, such as student study teams (Knotek, in press). In such settings, a consultant may have the tasks of collaborating in problem-solving and participating as a professional with some (usually lesser) degree of responsibility for a client, while simultaneously also acting in the role of consultant. Consultation occurs through the collaborative process as the consultant, using the basic consultation skill-sets, helps fellow members to develop new conceptualizations of the work problem and to expand their repertoire. This characterization of the utility of consultation in such circumstances appears to be generally in line with the stance adopted by Schulte and Osborne (1993) regarding consultation in general.

Third, consultee-centered consultation was originally one form of what Caplan called *mental health consultation*, which has often been incorrectly used as equivalent to consultee-centered consultation. The adjective *mental health* in consultee-centered mental health consultation reflected the fact that the origins of consultee-centered consultation were in settings where (a) clients had mental health disorders or personality idiosyncrasies, (b) the goal was the promotion of mental health in the client, and (c) there were interpersonal aspects of the consultee's work situation (Caplan, 1970). The intention was to promote mental health in the client and in the work setting, not necessarily in the consultee. However, the application of consultee-centered consultation over the years has been extended to settings such as schools and child-care centers where mental health is not the primary focus. In addition, because Caplan's theoretical perspective was psychodynamic, this orientation came to be seen as central to the approach. To many, *mental health* and *psychodynamic* were allied terms. More recently, theoretical approaches other than the psychodynamic have been used in the practice of consultee-centered consultation, and the automatic association to psychodynamic theory has been lost. As a result, authors in this volume have avoided the descriptor *mental health consultation* in an effort not to perpetuate a misconception. Another important issue in consultee-centered consultation, as well as in other forms, is that practice has gone beyond, and often before, empirical support (Dougherty, 2000). There is a lack of research that investigates the process and outcome of consultee centered consultation. The articles in this issue begin to establish a research base for practice.

A COMPARISON OF CONSULTEE-CENTERED CONSULTATION AND BEHAVIORAL CONSULTATION

Although there is a growing recognition that the various models of consultation have many similarities, consultee-centered consultation also varies from other forms. Any discussion about the ongoing development of consultee-centered consultation should first be placed in context within the big picture of the current practice of consultation. How does consultee-centered consultation compare to behavioral consultation? Behavioral consultation is considered to be the mostly widely practiced, understood, and researched form of consultation used in school settings (Conoley & Conoley, 1992; Gutkin & Curtis, 1999). The following discussion briefly considers important distinctions between behavioral and consultee-centered consultation.

Especially in comparison to behavioral consultation, consultee-centered consultation differs in its emphasis on the consultation relationship, its facilitation of both intrapsychic and interpersonal development in the consultee, and its lack of a core emphasis on behavioral technology (Dougherty, 2000). The relationship between the consultant and consultee is of central importance in consultee-centered consultation, so much so that consultation itself is not considered to happen unless the consultation relationship approximates some high degree of nonhierarchical status. The name *consultee-centered* consultation itself reflects the core focus of the consultation relationship, which is predicated on facilitating change in the conceptual understandings of the consultee. While the expectation exists that clients will ultimately be better served through consultation, the prime goal of this type is to reframe consultees' knowledge and reconceptualize their understanding of the work problem. Consultee-centered consultation seeks to facilitate change through the interpersonal process of the relationship, and can be considered as open with respect to the content discussed during consultation. In this form of consultation, depending upon the situation, the content discussed may range from behavioral modifications to instructional match to cognitive developmental milestones. In contrast, behavioral consultation is primarily defined by its emphasis on the use of behavioral technology and the systematic structure of consultation.

Another dimension on which consultee-centered consultation varies from behavioral consultation is the prescriptiveness of the form of the problem-solving process. Consultee-centered consultation is less prescriptive in that the outcome of consultation is not known in advance. The consultant is responsible for directing the process, but not for directing the content or the evolving solution to the consultation dilemma. The consultant does not advocate in advance any particular intervention or way of resolving the consultee's problem. As plans for action are developed during the process, the consultee is free to accept or reject options or suggestions as they occur. Both the consultant and the consultee are free to change their representations and presentations of the situation as the process progresses, and as such, the stages of problem solving are less well-structured and linear. Behavior consultation often has more finely prescribed problem-solving stages (Gutkin & Curtis, 1999).

Additionally, consultee-centered consultation aims to be non-hierarchical. In many forms of consultation, including behavioral, the consultant is more often in the role of expert in relation to the consultee and is in the position of offering advice. The consultant uses this influence based on the expert status to lead the consultation process and to generate potential solutions within a range of behavioral parameters. Although status differences are inevitable, the consultee-centered consultant works to create an egalitarian relationship by explicitly recognizing the consultee's expertise and making it the basis of a relationship among equals. Efforts are made to downplay status based on role and to recognize expertise where it exists.

Neither form of consultation is pure, and in reality the two approaches have many things in common. All describe a problem-solving relationship between the consultant and the consultee with the focus on the client. However, consultee-centered consultation places a heightened emphasis on the consultant–consultee relationship, on the goal of evoking conceptual change, and on the improvement of the consultee's working effectiveness with other clients.

THE SPECIAL ISSUE

This special issue will address the three core issues of theoretical base, the consultant's line of responsibility, and application in educational settings. Sandoval's (this issue) article presents a theoretical perspective on consultee-centered consultation from cognitive-change theory and constructivist notions. As Taylor (2001, p. 233) observes, "Theory without practice is empty; practice without theory is blind."

Hylander (this issue) describes grounded theory as a fruitful methodology to elucidate the dynamics of consultation and her application of this approach to the study of consultee-centered consultation. The remaining three articles each present concepts and results from empirical investigations that examine the process of consultee-centered consultation in the context of school settings. Webster, Knotek, Babinski, Rogers, and Barnett (this issue) present a study of the consultant's use of questions to improve coherency and mediate consultee's conceptual development. Knotek, Rosenfield, Gravois, and Babinski (this issue) present a study that investigates the consultant's use of orderly reflection to promote consultee's conceptual change during instructional consultation. Finally, Ingraham (this issue) presents a study in which novice consultants explore cultural hypotheses with experienced teacher consultees. We hope the reader will form a new and more complex view of consultee-centered consultation as a result of this special issue.

REFERENCES

Brown, D., Pryzwansky, W. B., & Schulte, A. C. (2001). *Psychological consultation: Introduction to theory and practice (5th ed.).* Boston: Allyn & Bacon.

Caplan, G. (1970). *Theory and practice of mental health consultation.* New York: Basic Books.

Caplan, G., & Caplan, R. B. (1993). *Mental health consultation and collaboration.* San Francisco: Jossey-Bass.

Conoley, J. C., & Conoley, C. W. (1992). *School consultation: Practice and training (2nd ed.).* Needham Heights, MA: Allyn & Bacon.

Dougherty, A. M. (2000). *Psychological consultation and collaboration in school and community settings (3rd ed).* Belmont, CA: Wadsworth.

Gutkin, T. B., & Curtis, M. J. (1999). School-based consultation theory and practice: The art and science of indirect service delivery. In C. R. Reynolds & T. B. Gutkin(Eds.), *The handbook of school psychology* (3rd ed., pp. 598–637). New York: Wiley.

Knotek, S. E. (in press). Development through discourse: Speech genres as pathways to conceptual change. In N. M. Lambert, I. Hylander, & J. Sandoval (Eds.), *Consultee-centered consultation: Improving the quality of professional services in schools and community organizations.* Mahwah, NJ: Lawrence Erlbaum Associates, Inc.

Lambert, N. M., Hylander, I., & Sandoval, J. (Eds.). (2003). *Consultee-centered consultation: Improving the quality of professional services in schools and community organizations.* Mahwah, NJ: Lawrence Erlbaum Associates, Inc.

Pryzwansky, W. B. (1977). Collaboration or consultation: Is there a difference? *Journal of Special Education, 11,* 179–182.

Schulte, A. C., & Osborne, S. S. (1993, April). What is collaborative consultation? The eye of the beholder. In D. Fuchs (Chair) *Questioning popular beliefs about collaborations consultation.* Symposium conducted at the annual meeting of the Council for Exceptional Children, San Antonio, TX.

Taylor, M. C. (2001). *The moment of complexity: Emergent network culture.* Chicago: University of Chicago Press.

West, J. F., & Idol, L. (1993). The counselor as a consultant in a collaborative school. *Journal of Counseling and Development, 71,* 673–683.

Steven E. Knotek is an Assistant Professor in the School Psychology Program at the University of North Carolina at Chapel Hill. His research interests include school-based problem-solving teams, communication processes in consultation, and pre-referral interventions.

Jonathan Sandoval is Professor of Education at the University of California, Davis, and is a former President of APA's Division of School Psychology. He has taught consultation to school psychology students for three decades and written for journals on the topic. In addition to consultation, his research interests include issues in applied measurement, the prevention of school crisis, the training of education professionals, and the promotion of mental health in schools.

JOURNAL OF EDUCATIONAL AND PSYCHOLOGICAL CONSULTATION, 14(3&4), 251–261

Constructing Conceptual Change in Consultee-Centered Consultation

Jonathan Sandoval

University of California, Davis

A central tenant of consultee-centered consultation is that the consultee is always an active agent in the consultation process, not a passive receiver of transmitted information. Both participants will be constructing new understandings during consultation. The consultant can facilitate consultation by asking questions to illuminate the consultee's current theory of what is causing the consultation predicament. Next, the consultant and consultee might explore how the consultee's theory is inadequate to explain this and other cases. When a new theory is generated, it must be an understandable substitute explanation. It must be an intelligible, coherent, and plausible explanation. Finally, the new conceptualization must be parsimonious and efficacious in working with future clients as well as the current client and problem.

Change is always a goal in consultation. Consultees wish to see change in a client's behavior or attitude, and may also wish to change their professional approach to working with the client. In consultee-centered consultation, there is the added notion that change is likely to occur in the consultee's and consultant's understanding of the consultation problem or dilemma, and that this change improves the working relationship of the consultee. Change is warranted, whenever the usual ways of thinking and acting do not have the desired effect.

Correspondence should be addressed to Jonathan Sandoval, School of Education, 1 Shields Avenue, University of California, Davis, Davis, CA 95616–8579. E-mail: Jhsandoval@ucdavis.edu

CONCEPTUAL CHANGE

Even as children, we develop naive conceptualizations and theories for how the world works. Our conceptualizations shift and become more sophisticated as we grow older as a result of observation, experience, and formal instruction. Once we have arrived at an understanding as an adult, our conceptualizations become set and remarkably difficult to change. In Piaget's (1950) terms, when faced with new information we are inclined to assimilate new information into existing schema. Ausubel (1963) describes the process of subsuming new information into older conceptions without fundamentally changing them, and cognitive theorists describe how we are more likely to use new information to confirm biases, rather than to challenge them (Tversky & Kahneman, 1974).

Theorists and researchers have found that for change and new learning to occur, four conditions identified by Posner, Strike, Hewson, and Gertzog (1982) must be present: (a) a dissatisfaction with existing conceptions, (b) a new conception that is intelligible, (c) a new conception that is initially plausible, and (d) a new conception that is fruitful in that it suggests the possibility of solving additional problems or explaining additional phenomena. If these conditions are part of an instructional program, students will accommodate, in the Piagetian sense, and change conceptual schema rather than assimilate new information into their old ones (Piaget, 1950). In this article I will argue that these same conditions must be present to bring about change in consultation.

CONCEPTUAL CHANGE IN CONSULTATION

Naive Conceptions

For the consultant focusing on the consultee, the first task is to identify existing conceptualizations. In consultation we must accept that a consultee, upon entering consultation, often has a conception of why a client behaves the way he or she does. However, acting on this conception, the consultee has not been successful. This lack of success often is what brings the consultee to consultation: The consultee's construction of the situation, if not naive, is at least not working to permit the consultee to be effective with the client. The task facing the consultant is to explore with the consultee new ways of theorizing about the problems and puzzles facing the consultee that will lead to productive ways for the consultee to serve the client. The consultant must begin by determining the consultee's understanding of the client's situation and the consultee's theory about why the problem exists.

Helping Consultees Tell Their Story

Consultees usually begin the consultation conversation by presenting a work problem or dilemma. The consultant assists by actively listening to the consultees' presentation of their story. To facilitate the presentation, the consultee restates information, reflects feelings, and summarizes the presentation thus far (see Benjamin, 1987, for a discussion of active listening). Consultants ask questions to clarify their own understanding of the consultees' conceptualization. In active listening, the goal is to understand the consultee's presentation meanwhile separating it, as necessary, from the consultant's own understanding, which may be different. The consultant may well be able to offer a different characterization or presentation after listening, but must acknowledge the legitimacy of the consultee's presentation.

Asking for consultation can be an anxiety producing event because consultees may feel they are acknowledging failure as professionals. As Caplan points out, it is important to respond to consultees nonverbally by showing interest while maintaining a relaxed, calm posture, and verbally by acknowledging the problem as a difficult one (Caplan & Caplan, 1993). Berlin (1977) argues that such a calm approach communicates to consultees that human problems are difficult, but not impossible to solve, and models a rational problem-solving approach for the consultee. That the consultant is not shocked or repelled by the dilemma is reassuring to the consultee.

Questions and Conceptual Change

A critical early step in the consultation process is problem identification, following relationship building, and maintaining rapport through active, empathic listening. Typically the consultant helps in the problem-identification process by asking questions to elicit the consultee's view of the consultation dilemma. At this point, questions may go beyond those needed for clarification. Guvå (1999) has suggested a number of questions to use in the process of problem-identification:

Questions that focus on the client's problem:
What is the problem with x? How old is x? What you mean is that x?

Questions that focus on the history of the client and problem:
    When did it start? What were some critical past incidents? What had you heard about x before you met him?

Questions that focus on the concrete here and now:
    Can you tell me when during the school day the client is at his worst? What did he do and how did others react?

Questions that focus on the consultee's explanations:
    Why do you think this is so? Is there something that can help us understand the client? What do you think is going on?

Questions that focus on the consultee's picture of the client:
    What does the client look like?

Questions that focus on the consultee's fantasies about the future:
    What do you think will happen if nothing is done?

Questions that focus on other imaginations (ghosts) of importance:
    Have you met similar problems before?

Questions that focus on the consultee's expectations of the consultant:
    What did you expect me to do for you when you asked for my assistance?

Questions such as these are very helpful in illuminating the consultee's initial theory (or theories) of human behavior in general, and specific theory of what is causing the consultation predicament. Most of the consultant's questions are open-ended (questions requiring an elaborated response) as opposed to closed questions (questions that can be answered yes or no; Benjamin, 1987). Open-ended questions, along with responses such as reflections and restatements, allow the consultee to explore the problem more easily, and communicate that the consultant is listening carefully to what is being said. The answers to all of these questions permit the consultant to view the consultee's understanding of the problem and the underlying theories of behavior. An important goal of consultation is to understand the consultee's initial representation of the problem. Equally important to the process, the answer to questions such as the ones previously posed will also provide the consultant with information to be used in also forming his or her own conceptualization of the situation. The consultant's construction of the problem frequently may be different from the consultee's.

Another useful question to ask of all consultees is "What have you tried to address the problem?" This question has several virtues. It permits the consultant to understand how the consultee has translated her or his theory into action. Actions often reveal theories that are not explicitly stated. Of course this question permits the consultant to avoid the trap of suggesting an action that has already been tried. It also permits statements of one downsmanship, as advocated by Caplan & Caplan (1993), in which the consultee's skill or initiative may be acknowledged.

Bergan and Kratochwill have also produced a well-known set of questions in an interviewing protocol which has also proven useful to many consultants (Bergan, 1977; Bergan & Kratochwill, 1990). These questions are particularly useful in building a consultant and consultee representation of the dilemma from a behavioral perspective, which may be one of several perspectives held by the consultant. The protocol functions to focus attention specifically and carefully on the client's behavior and the circumstances surrounding problem interactions between the consultee and client. Such an examination is useful in that it supplements the focus on the consultee's understanding and may lead to alternative conceptualizations.

Consultant Leads in Consultation

The consultant does not just ask questions and reflect on or restate what the consultee has said. At some point, the consultant will be able to define the problem from the consultee's point of view in a way that the consultee agrees is accurate. However, the consultant does offer other observations coming from his or her point of view or perspective. The statements may be termed *consultation leads*.

Leads may have many purposes. They may be designed to create cognitive dissonance, to reframe the facts presented, or to offer another conceptualization to the consultee. When the purpose is to create dissonance, the comments may be to point out or search for anomalous data, to comment on what is missing or unexplained in the consultee's statements of the problem, or to note contradictions in what has been said. Examples of consultant leads are "You describe the child as being x but you also describe him as being y—how do these go together?" "One explanation is that x causes y, but I suppose another is that y causes x." and "Could x be operating in this situation?"

Consultant comments or observations as leads come from the consultant's point of view. They originate in the consultant's representation and serve to either support it or solicit information needed to create a new representation of the problem. In addition to creating dissonance, they may also reframe the problem by reorganizing the information presented by the consultee. Using the same facts to reorganize information may also reorder cause and effect, or introduce new ideas to be discussed and verified.

The consultant may wish to use an anecdote, a metaphor, or a parable to introduce a new idea. The experienced consultants can offer stories of other consultees or their own experiences in another setting to make a point. Information presented in this way is often easier, and less threatening to hear on the part of the consultee, assuming the consultee is able to see the analogy and identify with the actor (Davis & Sandoval, 1978).

ACCESSIBLE REASONING AND CONCEPTUAL CHANGE

Argyris and Schön (1996) argue that in interpersonal problem solving, a key skill of the consultant is making explicit to the consultee their own conceptualization of the problem drawn from the information that has emerged from the consultation interview. That is, the consultant makes his or her reasoning accessible to the consultee (Monsen & Frederickson, 2002), and, more importantly, offers up the conceptualization for discussion and debate. Conceptions must be openly examined, tested, and falsified, if need be. To be tested, however, the conceptions must first be organized in hypothetical form. The testing may range from recollections, thought experiments, and actual trials of interventions with the client. The information used must be valid and objective. The discussion and testing must be done in a way that does not put the consultee or consultant on the defensive. Such a discussion requires great interpersonal skill, needless to say. As an example, a consultant might conclude: "From what you have said, I am wondering if what you describe is a result of the child being distractible, or if it is the case that the assignments are too difficult for him? I notice that he is not distractible during social studies or other subjects. This goes along with what you have said about copying other children when you give seat work. Is there a way to check this idea out?" Here the consultant is introducing a new train of thought along with a hypothesis to be tested.

Consultants also will be engaging in conceptual change. They will begin to form an internal representation of the consultation problem as they gather information. Their representation will no doubt be guided by their theories of human behavior. Most psychologist consultants will have several theories to explore and use to understand the problem situation. They may use social behavioral theory, developmental theory, attachment theory, psychodynamic theory, or many more, to make sense of the data presented. As they wrestle with the problem along with the consultee, they should constantly challenge their own theory-based constructions and be willing to shift representations and theories, if warranted, to contribute to the generation of a possible solution for the consultation dilemma.

THE CHANGE PROCESS

As the process evolves, the consultant and consultee will likely explore how the consultee's construction is inadequate to explain this and other cases. By the presentation of anomalous data—pointing out where the theory does not work and highlighting dissonant evidence not predicted by the consultee's framework—the consultant helps build dissatisfaction with the current explanatory theory. When a new theory is generated during consultation, it must be an understandable substitute. It must be intelligible, coherent, and internally consistent and must seem like a plausible explanation. Finally, the new idea must seem to have widespread applicability—it should be elegant, parsimonious, and efficacious in working with future clients and problems as well as the current client and problem. It should explain more of the observed facts of the case than the previous theory. The focus will be on anomalies, or how existing notions about the problem fail to explain the situation or produce interventions.

Eventually a new theory will be produced by the consultation. The new conceptualization may be proposed by the consultant or the consultee (or consultees, if it is a group consultation). Often analogies and metaphors will be used to introduce the new ideas and conceptualization and make them intelligible to both the consultant and consultee. For example, the child's behavior may be compared to a character in a movie, a book, or other cultural icon. References may be made to interactions among adults to illuminate interactions among children. Although analogies may be useful initially, it is important to be sure that the correct features are abstracted from the analogy and transferred to the new theory. (In the above example it should be made clear that adults are not children, and their thinking may not resemble a child's).

Unlike teaching, where the goal is often to bring the learner to an understanding of phenomena determined in advance by the teacher, the goal in consultation is not necessarily to have the consultee adopt the understanding of the consultant. Instead, the intent is for there to be a mutual construction of a conceptualization that fits the situation and permits action. This openness to mutual reconstruction makes the understanding that is the outcome of consultation unknown and unpredictable, but also makes the process enjoyable and challenging.

As consultants, we also see and often hope to observe paradigm shifts in our consultees. We hope that as an outcome of consultation, our consultees come to understand their clients in a new way which enables them to be helpful in their professional roles. In a sense, consultation can be an important tool for professional development, although consultees do not come with this in mind.

THEME INTERFERENCE AND CONCEPTUAL CHANGE

Caplan (1963) has identified four major categories of difficulty that bring a consultee to consultation: (a) lack of understanding of the psychological factors in the case; (b) lack of skills or resources to deal with the problems involved; (c) lack of professional objectivity in handling the case; and (d) lack of confidence and self-esteem due to fatigue, illness, inexperience, youth, or old age. Lack of understanding may indicate a missing conceptualization or a naive idea about the causes of the problem with a client, and lack of objectivity may indicate a conceptualization (or theme) that is mistaken or emotionally charged and in need of changing. Caplan recommends that theme interference reduction be used to address consultee problems of lack of objectivity, but acknowledges that this technique has not been endorsed by many consultants, particularly school-based practitioners (Caplan, Caplan, & Erchul, 1995).

A theme is "A conflict related to actual life experience or to fantasies that has not been satisfactorily resolved (and that) is apt to persist in a consultee's preconscious or unconscious as an emotionally toned cognitive constellation" (Caplan & Caplan, 1993, p. 122). Caplan suggests that in many cases, themes, like neutrally toned schema, interfere with effective problem solving but are even more difficult to address because of the negative affect. He describes how themes may be understood as syllogisms that the consultee has constructed, consisting of an initial category and an inevitable outcome. In consultation, these themes must be shown to be inadequate before new ways of working with and conceptualizing the client will emerge. Theme interference techniques include (a) demonstrating that the inevitable outcome is only one logical possibility and that other outcomes are more likely than the dreaded one, and (b) avoiding giving nonverbal validation to the theme outcome. These techniques of theme interference reduction may be viewed as attempts at conceptual change inasmuch as they attempt to change syllogisms constructed by the consultee. Perhaps considering theme interference reduction as a process of conceptual change, as well as recognizing the possibility that consultees do have *some sort* of theory about client behavior when they seem to lack understanding will be a fruitful way of viewing collaborative work.

Instead of offering a different conceptualization, however, the attempt with themes is to elaborate them to make them more plausible and fruitful for working with other clients. Anomalous data may be brought in to indicate how the initial category did not lead to the inevitable outcome. As Caplan suggests, the emphasis should be on how the theory is inadequate, not on how the theory is inapplicable to the particular client (Caplan & Caplan, 1993). There will be no motive to change the theory if it is perceived as not applying to the client.

It must be pointed out that sometimes consultee's difficulties of Caplan's lack of understanding (Caplan & Caplan, 1993) really exist because the consultee has no theory or conception. Some consultees are at a loss to explain behaviors or situations, and need to be helped to gain knowledge. Whether or not the consultant supplies the needed knowledge or refers the consultee to other sources depends on many factors having to do with the organizational structure of the institution in which the consultee works.

CONCLUSION

A central tenant in the constructivist learning theory is that the learner is always an active agent in the learning process, not a passive participant receiving transmitted information (Piaget, 1950). Translated into consultation theory, the consultee as well as the consultant must be active participants in the consultation process, and we must recognize that in consultation both participants will be constructing new understandings of the consultation dilemma (Cobern, 1993; Sandoval, 1996).

Henning-Stout (1994) has called for more research on the discourse of expert consultants, particularly those who are consultee-centered. Researchers such as Hylander (this issue) and Knotek, Rosenfield, Gravois, and Babinski (this issue) have begun to do so. I believe that effective consultants will be found to be engaged with their consultees in a process of conceptual change. Looking for conceptual change may in fact become a useful outcome variable for evaluating the consultation process. Conceptual change can be assessed by examining the transcripts of the consultation dialogue, by asking consultees explicitly to describe their theory of the client's behavior at different times, by asking them to think aloud about a similar client, and even by asking them to make pictorial models of the systems surrounding the consultation problem (Sandoval, 2004). If this were to be done, I believe consultees would shift, as do novices when they become experts, to more complex, deep, and differentiated models of the phenomena they encounter (deGroot, 1965). Deep and complex thinking on the part of the consultee and consultant should be a goal of the consultation process.

REFERENCES

Argyris C. & Schön , D. A. (1996). *Organizational learning II: Theory, method and practice*. Reading, MA: Addison-Wesley.

Ausubel, D. P. (1963). *The psychology of meaningful verbal learning: An introduction to school learning*. New York: Grune & Stratton.

Benjamin, A. (1987). *The helping interview with case illustrations*. Boston: Houghton Mifflin.

Bergan, J. R. (1977). *Behavioral consultation*. Columbus, OH: Merrill.

Bergan, J. R., & Kratochwill, T. R. (1990). *Behavioral consultation and therapy*. New York: Plenum.

Berlin, I. (1977). Lessons learned in 25 years of mental health consultation to schools. In S.C. Plog & P.I. Almed (Eds.), *Principles and techniques of mental health consultation* (pp. 23–48). New York: Plenum.

Caplan, G. (1963). Types of mental health consultation. *American Journal of Orthopsychiatry, 33*, 470–481.

Caplan, G., & Caplan, R. B. (1993). *The theory and practice of mental health consultation*. (2nd ed.). San Francisco: Jossey-Bass.

Caplan, G., Caplan, R. B., & Erchul, W. P. (1995). A contemporary view of mental health consultation: Comments on *Types of mental health consultation* by Gerald Caplan (1963). *Journal of Educational and Psychological Consultation, 6*, 23–30.

Cobern, W. W. (1993). Constructivism. *Journal of Educational and Psychological Consultation, 4*, 105–112.

Davis, J. & Sandoval, J. (1978). Metaphor in group mental health consultation. *Journal of Community Psychology, 6*, 374–382.

De Groot, A. D. (1965). *Thought and choice in chess*. The Hague, Netherlands: Mouton.

Guvå, G. (1999). Teachers ask for help, not for consultation. In I. Hylander (Chair), *Explorations in process in practice*. (Seminar proceedings). Stockholm: 2nd International Seminar on Consultee-centered consultation.

Henning-Stout, M. (1994). Consultation and connected knowing: What we know is determined by the questions we ask. *Journal of Educational and Psychological Consultation, 5*, 5–21.

Monsen, J. J., & Frederickson, N. (2002). Consultant problem understanding as a function of training in interviewing to promote accessible reasoning. *Journal of School Psychology, 40*, 197–212.

Piaget, J. (1950). *The psychology of intelligence*. London: Routledge & Kegan Paul.

Posner, G. P., Strike, K. A., Hewson, P. W., & Gertzog, W. A. (1982). Accommodation of a scientific conception: Toward a theory of conceptual change. *Science Education, 66,* 211–227.

Sandoval, J. (1996). Constructivism, consultee-centered consultation and conceptual change. *Journal of Educational and Psychological Consultation, 7,* 89–97.

Sandoval, J. (2004). Evaluation issues and strategies in consultee-centered consultation. In Lambert, N. M., Hylander, I., & Sandoval, J. (Eds.), *Consultee-centered consultation: Improving the quality of professional services in schools and community organizations,* Mahwah, NJ: Lawrence Erlbaum Associates, Inc.

Tversky, A., & Kahneman, D. (1974). Judgment under uncertainty: Heuristics and biases. *Science, 185,* 483–492.

Jonathan Sandoval is Professor of Education at the University of California, Davis, and is a former President of APA's Division of School Psychology. He has taught consultation to school psychology students for three decades and written for journals on the topic. In addition to consultation, his research interests include issues in applied measurement, the prevention of school crisis, the training of education professionals, and the promotion of mental health in schools.

JOURNAL OF EDUCATIONAL AND PSYCHOLOGICAL CONSULTATION, 14(3&4), 263–280

Toward a Grounded Theory of the Conceptual Change Process in Consultee-Centered Consultation

Ingrid Hylander
Linköping University

This article argues that a grounded-theory research methodology is a useful and fruitful tool to explore important questions in consultation and to generate new conceptualizations and theory (Glaser & Strauss, 1967). The grounded-theory approach is described and illustrated with examples from Hylander's research on consultee-centered consultation as practiced in Sweden. The result is a substantive theory about change processes. The theoretical research approach presented in this article makes it possible to further explore processes of consultation that have not been previously examined.

The purpose of this article is to discuss how a theory-generating research methodology can be used to generate theory about change in the consultation process (Glaser, 1978; Glaser & Strauss, 1967; Strauss & Corbin, 1990). Examples are given from a grounded-theory study focused on consultee-centered consultation in schools, preschools, and child daycare settings. The study is reported more extensively in a Swedish dissertation (Hylander, 2000).

Consultee-centered consultation is a common consultation model in Swedish schools, preschools, and childcare institutions. It is based upon and has evolved from Gerald Caplan's writings (Caplan, 1963, 1964, 1970; Caplan & Caplan, 1993, 1995) and the work of Gunilla Guvå (1989, 1992, 1995, 1999, 2001) and others (Brodin, 1999, 1995; Hylander, 2000; Thörn, 1999). When consultation came into use in Sweden 20–25 years

Correspondence should be addressed to Ingrid Hylander, Department of Behavioral Sciences, Linköping University, 58283, Linköping, Sweden. E-mail: inghy@ibv.liu.se

ago, consultants mainly used psychodynamic theory to frame their understandings of the process. Today there are several other theories that have been influential in forming the practice of consultee-centered consultation. Most important are systemic theory (Bateson, 1979), constructivistic theory (Anderson & Golishian, 1998; Berger & Luckman, 1967), ecological conceptualizations (Bronfenbrenner, 1979), object-relation theory (Winnicott, 1971), self-psychology (Brodin & Hylander, 1997; Stern, 1985), developmental theories (Piaget, 1968, 1971; Vygotsky,1970, 1978), organizational theories (Argyris & Schön 1974, 1978), and theories of reflective thinking (Andersen, 1994). The tradition of consultee-centered consultation is now a well-established practice in Sweden. This praxis has developed independently (up to 1989) along the same lines as the consultee-centered consultation approach being taught and developed at Berkeley (Lambert, Sandoval, & Corder, 1975; Lambert, Yandell, & Sandoval, 1975; Sandoval, 1999; Sandoval & Lambert, 1987). The core of this praxis is the focus on *process*, or the interactions between the consultant and the consultee, and the consultee and the clients. Conceptualizations of the consultation process are not drawn from just one theory, but spring from several different theories of behavior, communication, and organization. Consultee-centered consultation is a *nonprescriptive* model of consultation. Nonprescriptive means leaving the responsibility to accept or reject suggestions to the consultee. The consultee is in charge of the solution to the problem and of all the interventions subsequently implemented. The consultant is ready to constantly change his or her own representation of the problem and the way to solve it. Being *prescriptive* as consultant, on the other hand, (as in behavioral consultation) means being an expert in generating a solution to the problem. The consultant then maintains his or her own representation of the problem, wanting the teacher or consultee to assume the consultant's perspective.

The way in which consultee-centered consultation is typically implemented in Swedish childcare settings, preschools, and schools is by group consultation (Guvå, 1989; Hylander, 1995). The teachers meet with a psychologist between 1 and 1 ½ hr, every 3 or 4 weeks until the teachers say that they have solved the problem, they know how to handle it better, or that for some other reason they want to terminate. A consultation case usually ranges from two to seven sessions. Between the sessions the teachers make observations, conduct interviews or make other inquiries, the results of which are discussed with the psychologist. Later, the consultees implement different strategies that have emerged from the discussion in the consultation session. The actions taken and results are then evaluated in the following session.

RESEARCH ON CONSULTATION

During the middle of the 1980s there was a common agreement that earlier research on consultation had been lacking in rigor and had not answered vital questions or even posed meaningful questions (Meade, Hamilton & Yuen, 1982; Hughes, 1994; Pryzwansky 1986; Wiström, 1990). Few studies rendered theory that could explain what was happening in the consultation process (i.e., showing how the consultant's intervention relates to the consultee's interaction with the client and to the problem that originated the consultation).

Within the 1980s, interest grew in new perspectives and a common model for how to identify and define what should be investigated in consultation (Gallessich, 1985; Meade, Hamilton, & Yuen, 1982; Pryzwansky, 1986). Consultation articles with titles like *On the Verge of a Breakthrough* (Bardon, 1985) and *The Time has Come the Walrus Said* (Meade et al., 1982) foresaw new advancements in consultation practice and research. A clear description of practice and new conceptualizations of consultation processes across different perspectives and different settings were needed to facilitate coordinated consultation research. Those advancements have not materialized, and since the middle of the 1980s there has been a decline in theoretical writings and research on consultation practice other than in behavioral consultation. Theoretical and conceptual issues often apply only to prescriptive models of consultation (e.g., power and influence in consultation; Erchul, 1987, 1992; Erchul & Chewning 1990; Erchul & Martens, 1997). Experimental designs within consultation research have become much more rigorous and solid but focus almost exclusively on behavioral consultation (Bramlett & Murphy, 1998). Little work has been done on other forms of consultation, including consultee-centered consultation.

In other countries where consultee-centered consultation is a well-known practice there are but a few studies examining the consultation process, for example in Israel (Bar El, Mester, & Klein, 1982; Caplan & Caplan, 1995), Norway (Johannessen, 1990, 1999), Sweden (Brodin & Hylander, 1995; Guvå, 1999, 2001; Hylander, 2000; Wiström, Hanson, Qvarnström, & Westerlund, 1995), Russia (Pakhalian, 1990), and Greece (Hatzichristou, 1999). Lately, there is a new interest in exploring the complexity of the consultation practice using a wide variety of research methodologies (Henning-Stout, 1994; Meyers, 1995; Pryzwansky & Noblit, 1990; Rosenfield, 1991; Sandoval, 1999).

A THEORY-GENERATING RESEARCH METHODOLOGY

Consultee-centered consultation is a complex process. Thus, exploring simple relationships of cause and effect through the manipulation of single variables does not seem fruitful. What is needed is a research approach that can explore, describe, understand, and possibly explain the complexity of the consultee-centered consultation process. When conducting that kind of conceptual and explorative research, it is desirable to avoid a particular psychological theory of behavior, lest a theoretical perspective blind the researcher to important and new phenomena. Starting with one specific theory may also restrict the outcome of any study if the model of consultation is defined in specific terms at the onset of the study. Even if consultants refer to a common and specific model of consultation, consultants may not always do what they say they are doing and may engage in behaviors that they are not aware of during consultation. For example, in a Norwegian study of consultation in a preschool, Johannessen (1990) noted that there was a great gap between how consultation was described in theory and what it was like in real practice, as consultants did not follow a specific model of consultation. In order to discover new patterns, and possibly generate a new theoretical model for change in the consultation process, it is useful to start with an inductive approach. Grounded theory is such a research methodology.

Grounded theory is the theory-generating method developed by Glaser and Strauss (1967; Glaser, 1978, 1992; Stern, 1980, 1994; Strauss, 1987; Strauss & Corbin, 1990), who sought to find alternatives to the dominating deductive theory-testing model of research. Grounded theory is particularly suitable when a researcher wants to explore a new field or provide a new perspective on a well-established theory or area of study. It does not test a given theory to find out if it is valid or not, but explores raw data to discover new patterns that permit the generation of possibly new substantive theory.

The roots of grounded theory are within the philosophy of pragmatism and the theory of symbolic interactionism, traditions with links to social constructivism (Anderson & Goolishian, 1998; Annells, 1996; Berger & Luckman, 1967; Guvå & Hylander, 1998, 2003; Pidgeon & Henwood, 1997; Starrin, Larsson, Dahlgren, & Styrborn, 1991). Phenomena are studied from the perspective of the actors in the natural environment where they act. The concepts are created through interactions between the researcher and the empirical data. Although the concepts generated reflect the social acts, they are also constructions that acquire their symbols and meanings from the researcher (Blumer, 1969; Mead, 1934). In the investigation described in this paper, the method of focus group interviews was used with new information constructed during the interviews (Hylander, 1998; Morgan, 1997; Morgan & Kreuger, 1993). The raw data derived from observations, interviews, and the analyses of interactions were used to generate a substantive theory.

Applications to the Study of Consultation

A grounded-theory approach may be used to gain knowledge about change processes in consultee-centered consultation. A grounded-theory study does not start with a specific research question but a general question or just an interest in a field (Glaser, 1978). As the research progresses and the results provide new information, more distinct questions are asked.

The question I started out to explore was: What actually happens when a teacher (consultee) tells the consultant (psychologist) that the child she worried so much about is now doing much better and now she (i.e., the consultee) views the problem in a different way than previously? What has changed? The child, the understandings of the teacher, or the understandings of the consultant? Within the analyses of the data (and in accordance with the guidelines described below), much effort was spent on exploring the matter of what can be subject to change in consultation. It was discovered that the questions discussed here could be explored by focusing on changes of the presentation of the problem and the experience of change of the inner representation of that problem. The term *representation* came to be used for the internal conceptualizations of the problem brought to consultation. *Presentation*, in contrast, refers to all verbal statements and nonverbal behaviors with which a representation is presented in consultation. When consultees claim that the problem brought to consultation has been solved or that they can manage it by themselves, the consultee and the consultant have framed the problem in a different way. Such a change in representation, such a conceptual shift, is called a *turning*. This turning may be due to a conceptual change in the consultee as well as in the consultant (Sandoval, 1996). Most likely, this turning has been followed by a change in the consultee's way of understanding and interacting with the client, which in turn brings about a change in the client. However, consultants may never be sure of what has shifted. The only thing they will know for certain is whether the consultees' way of presenting their own representations of the problem has changed. Thus, a successful consultation process ends with a different presentation *and* representation of the problem—a turning.

When the process of data analyses had reached this far, more specific research questions were stated: (a) How can patterns of change in consultee's representations and presentations of a problem be identified, understood, and explained; (b) what aspects of the interaction between the consultant and the consultee can help in understanding and explaining changes in the consultee's representations and presentations of a problem; and (c) how can patterns of interactions between the consultee's presentations and representations of a problem, and the consultant's presentation and representation of the problem, help in understanding and explaining when the consultation process is stuck and no change occurs? Grounded-theory methodology was used to answer these important questions.

Theoretical Sampling

Theoretical sampling is used in grounded theory to collect the data, which means that the sampling process continues throughout the investigation and is guided by the emerging theory (Glaser, 1978; Strauss & Corbin, 1990). When new information is needed in a study to ground the concepts (i.e., saturate the categories) or understand the patterns that appear, new data are collected or old data are used in a new way. Sample data are initially collected from individuals who are in situations where the phenomenon under study is likely to exist. Thus, research conducted to study change in consultee-centered consultation should focus on experienced consultants working in frameworks where consultee-centered consultation is a common and accepted form of service delivery. In later stages, participants working in other situations that challenge the generalizability of the phenomenon being studied may also be selected. This data gathering approach means that it is not always possible to relate the origin of a certain concept to specific data but the concepts may always be illustrated by excerpts from the data.

The theoretical concepts derived in Hylander's (2000) study of consultee-centered consultation were based on data from focus groups, audio taped consultation sessions, interviews, and responses to questionnaires from consultants and consultees in schools, preschools, and daycare settings. The samples consisted of the following four data sources.

Focus groups.   Focus groups were conducted with five consultants employed in daycare settings and preschools. This group of consultants were chosen because they had extensive experience in conducting consultee-centered consultation. Seven psychologists with extensive experience in other consultation approaches within different settings (e.g., organizations, private enterprise, schools, child daycare setting, child healthcare settings) also participated in a second set of focus groups. A third focus group consisted of five psychologists with extensive experience in providing consultee-centered consultation in schools, daycare settings, and preschools. This group was a strategic choice to guarantee experiences from school consultation within a consultee-centered frame of reference.

The main question to the participants in the first set of focus groups was: "Can you identify change in consultations and if so, how do you describe it?" Change was not defined, but illustrated by a general case:

> Teachers consult a psychologist about a child who the teachers found so difficult that they did not know what to do or how to handle the child. They are upset and give a very negative picture of the child and make the consultant concerned about the outcome of the case. The next time the consultant arrives the teachers calmly discuss the child's progress and say that everything is much better.

The participants in the focus groups recognized this as a typical case and said that they could identify what changes occurred within the process, but in doing so they described very different change phenomena. These phenomena were later coded as different types of change in consultation. However, in order to collect data about the *causes* of the changes described in the focus groups, participants were asked to join another focus group and to bring concrete cases where they had identified that a change had occurred. The focus groups rendered 20 consultation cases in daycare settings, preschools, and schools that were used in the data analysis. The consultees were teachers and childcare assistants. Most of the cases were group consultations. The kinds of problems presented to the consultants represented a wide range of behavioral, relational, and developmental challenges such as aggressive and impulsive behaviors, autistic syndromes, selective mutism, mental retardation, temper tantrums, and parental neglect. All focus groups were audio-taped and transcribed.

Audio-taped consultation cases.   A total of 19 sessions from six consultants were analyzed. The consultants were all psychologists with more than 15 years of experience in consultee-centered consultation and the consultees were teams of teachers with different degrees of early-childhood training. The clients were four boys and two girls between the ages of 3 and 5 with a wide range of presenting problems (e.g., temper tantrums, aggressive behaviors, parental neglect, retarded development, over dependency on adults).

Interviews. Interviews were conducted with consultants and consultees from the audio-taped cases. The questions targeted the consultees' and consultants' experiences with previous consultation cases, descriptions of the present cases, and descriptions of the consultation process, with focus on the interactions and relationships between the consultees and the consultants. The consultants were interviewed individually. The consultees were interviewed within the same teams they had been in during their consultation cases. The interviews were audio-taped and transcribed.

Questionnaires. A total of 102 consultees completed a questionnaire. The purpose of the questionnaire was to evaluate the consultation program in a childcare setting in one city in Sweden (Brodin & Hylander, 1995). For the purposes of this study, only the open-ended questions were analyzed. They were comments to questions like "What did you think about the process of consultation now, after your consultation cases have ended?" "Did you think that the problem was solved or could be better handled as a result of consultation?" "Would you contact the consultant again if you had problems with a child?" "Did you learn anything that could be useful for other situations with other children?" The questionnaires were distributed to the consultees by mail.

Data Analysis

The research methodology in grounded theory actually consists of several different methods that include methods for sampling, methods for coding, and methods for analyses. The methodology is typically performed in two (Glaser, 1978) or three steps (Hallberg, 1992, 1994; Strauss & Corbin, 1990). Hylander used an elaborated version of the methodology that consisted of four steps (Guvå & Hylander, 2003): (a) from data to labeled indicators, (b) from labeled indicators to concepts, (c) from concepts to search for patterns, and (d) arriving at a theory. The four steps, with examples from patterns and theory presented in this article, are found in Table 1. For each step there is a method for sampling, a method for coding, and a method for comparative analyses. However, it is important to point out that even though grounded theory is described as a procedure of four steps, it is not a linear process. The research process may simultaneously include all the different steps of analysis in relation to different parts of data and different concepts, until the final integration. In the following sections, a presentation of the different steps with examples from Hylander's research is described.

From data to labeled indicators. Data are repeatedly coded and sorted by computer. Coded indicators make up categories that are also given codes. An *indicator* is a word or a phrase that gives an indication, a hint, or an idea about what is going on in the data. A *category* is a conglomeration of similar coded indications with a common label. Thus, a category is made up of coded indicators or subcategories of coded indicators. A *code* is the label that is given to an indicator or a category. A code may be an exact replica of what is said or an in vivo code (e.g., *magic turning*, a code that was used when consultees described a change that surprised them as they didn't know how it came about). A code may also be a word taken from the discipline in which the researcher works (e.g., *representation*), or from some other field (e.g., *weather-cock turning* [in vitro code], which Hylander used to label reversible turnings, defined as cases that seemed to have succesful solutions with problems emerging in the following consultation session). Every new code is compared to all other codes and categories of codes by constant comparison (Glaser, 1978). In this study, the comparison described here rendered a list of codes with 11 categories, with subcategories on 5 levels.

From labeled indicators to concepts. The code list is a tool for conceptualization and analysis; it constantly changes during the research process. For example, in this research study there were 11 different main versions of the code list before the final theory was developed. *Concepts* are saturated categories and have a distinctive meaning with a well-chosen code that gives a good description of the concept (e.g., *false turning*, defined as the presentation from the consultees that they now can handle the problem in a better way, even though that is not the case; in such cases consultees often wanted to stop working with the consultant or wanted to talk about something else). Categories are saturated when there are enough coded indica-

TABLE 1

Procedures in Grounded Theory as Applied to the Consultee-Centered Consultation Study of Turnings (Hylander, 2000)

Objectives	Samples	Coding	Comparative Analysis
Step 1 Labeled indicators	Open theoretical sample. Two focus groups with consultants.	Open coding. Coding indicators resulted in a list of 150 codes in 11 categories.	Sorting. Constant comparison between indicators and codes.
Step 2 Grounded concepts	Strategic sample. Third focus group with consultants. Second set of focus group interviews.	Conceptual coding. A coding list with subcategories on five levels. Turnings, tuning points, and shifts appear as main categories. Different kinds of turnings appear as grounded concepts.	Conceptual analysis. The variations within the concepts are analyzed.
Step 3 Patterns	Variational/relational sample. Inventories with consultees. Reported cases. Taped consultation sessions. Interview's.	Theoretical coding. Representations, presentations, movement, being stuck, closeness, and distance appear as theoretical codes relating concepts.	Pattern analysis. Diagrams and theoretical codes are used to describe relating concepts and their subcategories. Conceptual case stories are developed. Interactions of theoretical codes are described.
Step 4 Theoretical model	Selective sampling. Excerpts from the taped cases illustrating the oscillation between closeness and distance in the interactions between consultants and consultees are used to describe aspects of model.	Selective coding. The core process is identified as a process oscillating between closeness and distance to the original presentations and representations of the problem.	Integration. The different types of turnings are related to the core process.

tors that make up subcategories used to describe different aspects and dimensions of the category. The concepts are compared to each other to guarantee that concepts do not overlap and that there are vital differences between them.

From concepts to search for patterns.   The different concepts are linked to each other by theoretical codes and form patterns. A *theoretical code* may be a general concept or a graph that shows the relationships between concepts. Those strategies are helpful in uncovering patterns within the data. For example, in the present study it was discovered that closeness, distance, and movement were important theoretical codes that could be used to combine concepts to promote understanding of the interactions between the consultees and the consultants and the consultees and the clients, and how these interactions led to turnings.

Arriving at a theory.   The patterns are finally integrated into a model explaining the core process. The core process explains the core variable, which in a grounded-theory study is either the most important category or an interaction between several important categories. In the consultee-centered study the core variable was the turning of presentations and representations. The core process explaining these turnings was the oscillation between closeness and distance in the interactions between

1. The consultees and the clients.
2. The consultees and the consultants in relation to the originally presented problem.
3. The consultants' presentations and representations and the consultees' presentations and representations when shifting from being stuck to moving freely within the consultation process.

The constant comparisons and analysis in grounded theory should continuously be documented in memos. In the beginning of the research, the process memo consists of short notes about what category a coded indicator referred to or an idea about a category (Glaser, 1978; Strauss & Corbin, 1990). As concepts emerge, patterns and theory are elaborated; memos then turn up in theoretical discussions about hypotheses that have emerged. At the end of the process, memos are also sorted and made the basis for the research report.

Turnings

One research question I set out to answer was "How can patterns of change in consultee's representations and presentations of a problem be identified, understood, and explained?" The pattern of turnings is briefly presented in this section to illustrate how theory is derived from data.

The databases for turnings were primarily the six focus groups with consultants and the consultees' questionnaires. When different types of turnings emerged and they were coded and reconceptualized, they were then used to code the consultation cases presented in the second set of focus groups and in the audio-taped consultation cases.

After having discovered that the presentation and representations of a case were the major aspects of change in consultation that emerged, it was also understood that a successful consultation process ends with a different presentation and representation of the problem. Such a change in representation, such a conceptual shift, was coded as a turning. The next question to approach was "What did the presentations and representations consist of?" When consultees and consultants described a change, they gave examples of changed feelings (e.g., "It's a relief to discard all the bad feelings we have in regard to these children, then we become nicer and wiser"), changed cognitions (e.g., "We could see his behavior from a different angle, not just naughtiness and mischief"), and changed action tendencies (e.g., "I got many different ways of managing the problem illustrated [in consultation], I tried different ways until there was a result"). Thus, presentations and representations were described in terms of emotional, cognitive, and action tendency aspects. The outcome of a consultation process ideally is a turning of all these aspects. This is illustrated in the following example:

> Three teachers in a daycare setting contact a psychologist because they have problems with a 5-year-old boy who is aggressive with other children. The child has recently moved and came to the center. The teachers are worn out and have low self-esteem. Their affective arousal is high and they give very negative descriptions of the child. There are several boys in the group with behavioral problems who are acting out and being aggressive, and a couple of children with special needs. The parents of the other children are critical of the staff. The teachers don't want to go to work in the morning and they bring the problems with them when they go home. When they have shared their agony with the consultant, they give a less negative picture of the child. The consultant has little hope and feels discouraged because of the massive impact of the problems. The consultant discusses the possibility of making one of the teachers primarily responsible for the boy so that the other teachers can focus

on the other children. In the next consultation session the consultees' presentations are quite different. They are calm and reflective, give a positive picture of the boy and are aware of what they have done to make a change. The boy has calmed down. One of the teachers has approached the boy, giving him special attention, and discovering that he is very clever but has never been in a group setting before. The activities in the group are now more organized as the other two teachers have had more time for the other children. There are two more consultation sessions where the change is firmly established. In the last session, the teachers say that the boy is like a beaming star and they believe that he is going to do very well in school next year. (Focus group 2:2)

In this case, after the turning, the teachers present the child with a different emotional tone, a cognitive description, and a description of what they are doing. They are also aware and describe that their own representation of the problem is quite different. They have a positive picture of the child; they feel confident and have gone from being rather distant towards him to approaching him.

Teachers in this investigation said that some cases turned because they obtained a greater distance from the child and the child's problem, while other teachers said that the case turned when they approached the child. Moving between closeness and distance became a useful theoretical code to categorize the changes in the consultees' presentations of their relationships with the children.

VALIDATING A GROUNDED THEORY

It is important to emphasize that the resulting theory consists of hypotheses well-grounded in data but not verified in the hypothetico-deductive sense. Testing these hypotheses is a different matter and may become a task for later research. According to Kvale (1989), validation is built into the research process in the grounded-theory approach because verification is part of theory development and not some final outcome. It nevertheless seems relevant to discuss grounded theory according to different criteria of validity. Important for most qualitative studies are that results have credibility, consistency, and applicability. Glaser (1978) adds a fourth criterion: modifiability. *Credibility* is equivalent to empirical grounding or fit and implies that the study should be well-grounded in data and that concepts should have evolved from open coding and fit new data. *Consistency* or work means that concepts are generated and systematically related to each other, that there are several conceptual relations, and that the categories are well-developed and integrated into a core process (Glaser, 1978). A substantive theory should be relevant to the field from where it originated (i.e., *applicability*), which can be accomplished in consultation research by presenting the theory to audiences of psychological consultants and teachers. Objectivity and generalizability, important criteria for quantitative studies, have different implications for qualitative research. Instead of objectivity, a discourse criterion or communicative validity may be used (Kvale, 1989) to focus on how well the results can be explained in comparison to other possible alternative explanations. The theory that is the result of a grounded-theory study never claims to be the best explanation, but should relate to, and if relevant, should include parts of other possible theories. As the purpose is to create theory, still another criterion important in a grounded-theory study is that the theory is new and provides a new perspective on the phenomena studied. When the theory is applied to other settings or situations that differ from the original design, data that do not fit the theory should be analyzed and should constitute the bases for changes of or additions to the theory.

The research findings summarized in this article show that grounded theory is a useful research methodology to understand complex concepts about consultee-centered consultation. Focusing on change of presentations and representations is a fruitful way of exploring the problem of change target in researching consultee-centered consultation. It also opens up for exploration not only the consultee's conceptual change, but also the consultants' conceptual change. Using movement between closeness and distance as a theoretical concept in the analyses of what is happening between the consultee and the consultant, as well as between the consultee and the client, also seems a promising and new way to understand the consultation process. This opens up for study new aspects of the consultation process and for exploring the following questions:

- How do different types of problems, as presented by the consultee, end up in different types of turnings or no turnings at all?
- How do the interactions between the consultees and the consultants promote turnings?
- How is it possible for the consultant to change his or her presentations and representations of the problem to avoid getting stuck or getting out of being stuck in the consultation process?

These questions may be further investigated using the grounded-theory approach. My belief is that there is a need for using a great variety of research approaches to advance the conceptualization of consultation and thereby also explore and contrast the consultation approaches used around the world.

REFERENCES

Andersen, T. (1994). *Reflekterande processer. Samtal om samtalen* [Reflecting processes. Talking about dialogues]. Stockholm: Mareld.

Anderson, H., & Goolishian, H. (1998). Human systems as linguistic systems: Preliminary and evoking ideas about the implication for clinical theory. *Family Process 27*, 371–394.

Annells, M. (1996). Grounded theory method: Philosophical perspectives, paradigm of inquiry and postmodernism. *Qualitative Health Research, 6*, 379–393.

Argyris, C., & Schön, D. (1974). *Theory in practice*. San Fransisco: Jossey-Bass.

Argyris, C., & Schön, D. (1978). *Organisational learning*. Reading, MA: Addison-Wesley.

Bardon, J. (1985). On the verge of a breakthrough. *The Counseling Psychologist, 13*, 355–361.

Bar El, I., Mester, R., & Klein, H. (1982). Experience in community mental health consultation. *Israel Journal of Psychiatry Related Science, 19*, 173–180.

Bateson, G. (1979). *Mind and nature. A necessary unity*. Toronto, Canada: Bantam.

Berger, P. L., & Luckman, T. (1967). *The social construction of reality*. Garden City, NY: Anchor.

Blumer, H. (1969). *Symbolic interactionism: Perspective and method*. Englewood Cliffs, NJ: Prentice Hall.

Bramlett, K., & Murphy, J. (1998). School psychology perspectives on consultation: Key contributions to the field. *Journal of Educational and Psychological Consultation, 9*, 29–55.

Brodin, M. (1995). *Bilden av barnet I konsultationsprocessen. Bilden av ärendet I handledningsprocessen* [The picture of the child in the consultation process. The picture of the case in supervision]. (Uppsats för Ericastiftelsens handledarutbildning i konsultation, 1993–1995). Stockholm: Ericastiftelsen.

Brodin, M. (1999). An affect-theoretical approach to the consultation process, focused on the consultee's expression of what the client looks like. In I. Hylander & G. Guvå (Eds.), *Explorations in process in practice, 23–28*. (Seminar proceedings). Stockholm: 2nd International Seminar on Consultee-Centered Consultation.

Brodin, M., & Hylander, I. (1995). *Utvärdering av konsultationsärenden* [Assessment of consultation]. Lidingö: Lidingö Stad.

Brodin, M., & Hylander, I. (1997). *Att bli sig själv. Daniel Sterns teori i förskolans vardag* [To Become One Self. The theory of Daniel Stern applied to preschool practice]. Stockholm: Liber.

Bronfenbrenner, U. (1979). *The ecology of human development*. Cambridge, MA: Harvard University Press.

Caplan, G. (1963). Types of mental health consultation. *American Journal of Orthopsychiatry, 33*, 470–481.

Caplan, G. (1964). *Principles of preventive psychiatry*. New York: Basic Books.

Caplan, G. (1970). *The theory and practice of mental health consultation*. New York: Basic Books.

Caplan, G. & Caplan, R. (1993). *Mental health consultation and collaboration*. San Francisco: Jossey-Bass.

Caplan, G., & Caplan, R. (1995, May). *Recent advances in mental health consultation and collaboration*. Paper presented at the International Seminar on Consultee-centered Case Consultation, Hasselbacken, Stockholm.

Erchul, W. P. (1987). A relational communication analysis of control in school consultation. *Professional School Psychology, 2*, 113–124.

Erchul, W. P. (1992). On domination, cooperation, teamwork, and collaboration in school-based consultation. *Journal of Educational and Psychological Consultation, 3*, 363–366.

Erchul, W. P., & Chewning, T. G. (1990). Behavioral consultation from a request-centered relational communication perspective. *School Psychology Quarterly, 5*, 1–20.

Erchul, W. P., & Martens, B. K. (1997). *School consultation: Conceptual and empirical bases of practice.* New York: Plenum.

Gallessich, J. (1985). Towards a meta-theory of consultation. *The Counseling Psychologist, 13*, 363–354.

Glaser, B. (1978). *Theoretical sensitivity. Advances in the methodology of grounded theory.* San Francisco: Sociology Press.

Glaser, B. (1992). *Basics of grounded theory analyses: Emergence vs. forcing.* Mill Valley, CA: Sociology Press.

Glaser, B., & Strauss, A. (1967). *The discovery of grounded theory.* Chicago: Aldine.

Guvå, G. (1989). *Klientmysteriet. Ett fall för förskolepsykologen. Om personalinriktad fallkonsultation* [The mystery of the client. A case for the preschool psychologist. About consultee-centered case consultation]. (Sfph:s monografiserie nr 32.) Stockholm: Psykisk Hälsa.

Guvå, G. (1992). Om mellanområdet i konsultation [About the intermediate area in consultation]. *Psykisk Hälsa 3*, 205–210.

Guvå, G. (1995). *Professionsutveckling hos konsulter. Om konsultativ handledning och självutveckling* [The professional development of consultants. About consultative supervision and self development]. (FOG-Rapport No. 25). Linköpings universitet, Institutionen för Pedagogik och Psykologi.

Guvå, G. (1999). The first consultation session. How to meet a teacher who asks for help but not for consultation. In I. Hylander & G. Guvå (Eds.), *Explorations in process in practice, 39–44.* (Seminar proceedings). Stockholm: 2nd International Seminar on Consultee-Centered Consultation.

Guvå, G. (2001). *Skolpsykologers rolltagande. Överlämning och hantering av elevvårdsfrågor* [The role of school psychologists. Handling over and handling problems with individual students]. (Dissertation). Linköping: Linköpings Universitet. Institutionen för beteendevetenskap.

Guvå, G., & Hylander, I. (1998). *Att tillägna sig grounded theory* [Learning Grounded Theory]. (FOG-rapport nr 43). Linköping: Linköpings universitet. Institutionen för pedagogik och psykologi.

Guvå, G., & Hylander, I. (2003). *Grundad teori ett teorigenererande forskningsperspektiv* [Grounded Theory, a theory generating research perspective]. Stockholm: Liber.

Hallberg, L. (1992). *Hearing impairment, coping and perceived handicap, in middle-aged individuals with acquired hearing loss: An interactional perspective.* Unpublished doctoral dissertation. Gothenburg, Sweden: Gothenburg University, Department of Psychology.

Hallberg L. (1994). *En kvalitativ metod influerad av grounded theory-traditionen* [A qualitative method influenced by the Grounded Theory tradition]. Göteborg: Göteborgs universitet.

Hatzichristou, C. (1999). Alternative school psychological services: Development of a model linking theory, research and service delivery. In *Explorations in process in practice.* (Seminar proceedings) Stockholm: 2nd International Seminar on Consultee-Centered Consultation.

Henning-Stout, M. (1994). Consultation and connected knowing: What we know is determined by the question we ask. *Journal of Educational and Psychological Consultation, 5*, 5–22.

Hughes, J. N. (1994). Back to basics: Does consultation work? *Journal of Educational and Psychological Consultation, 1*, 77–84.

Hylander, I. (1995, May 5–7). *Evolvement of consultee-centered case consultation in Sweden.* Paper presented at The International Seminar on Consultee-Centered Case Consultation, Hasselbacken, Stockholm.

Hylander, I. (1998). *Fokusgrupper som kvalitativ datainsamlingsmetod* [Focus groups as a research method for collecting qualitative data]. (Fog-rapport nr 42). Linköping: Linköping University. Department of Behavioural Science.

Hylander, I. (2000). *Turning processes: The change of representations in consultee-centered case consultation.* Unpublished doctoral dissertation, Linköping University, Sweden.

Johannessen, E. (1990). *Gruppekonsultasjon med barnehagepersonale* [Group consultation with child care personnel]. Oslo: Barnevernsakademiet i Oslo. Statens speciallaerehögskole.

Johannessen, E. (1999). How to complicate the thinking of the consultee. In I. Hylander & G. Guvå (Eds.), *Explorations in process in practice, 69–74.* (Seminar proceedings). Stockholm: 2nd International Seminar on Consultee-Centered Consultation.

Kvale, S. (1989). To validate is to question. In S. Kvale (Ed.), *Issues of validity in qualitative research.* Lund, Sweden: Studentlitteratur.

Lambert, N., Sandoval, J., & Corder, R. (1975) Teacher perceptions of school-based consultants. *Professional Psychology, 6,* 204–216.

Lambert, N., Yandell, W., & Sandoval, J. (1975). Preparation of school psychologists for school-based consultation. A training activity and a service to community schools. *Journal of School Psychology, 13,* 68–76.

Mead, G. (1934). *Mind, self and society.* Chicago: University of Chicago Press.

Meade, C. J., Hamilton, M. K., & Yuen, R. K. W. (1982). Consultation research: The time has come the walrus said. *The Counseling Psychologist, 10,* 39–51.

Meyers, J. (1995). A consultation model for school psychological services: 20 years later. *Journal of Educational and Psychological Consultation, 6,* 73–81.

Morgan, D. (1997). *Focus groups as qualitative research* (Qualitative Research Methods Series No. 16). Thousands Oaks, CA: Sage.

Morgan, D., & Kreuger, R. (1993). When to use focus groups and why. In D. Morgan (Ed.), *Successful focus groups: Advancing the state of the art* (pp. 3–19). Newbury Park, CA: Sage.

Pakhalian, V. (1990). The work of the psychologist in preparing and conducting a pedagogical consultation. *Voprosy Psikhologii, 2,* 86–90.

Piaget, J. (1968). *Barnets själsliga utveckling.* Lund: Liber Läromedel.

Piaget, J. (1971). *The language and thought of the child.* London: Latiner Trend & Co.

Pidgeon, N., & Henwood, K. (1997). Using grounded theory in psychological research. In N. Hayes (Ed.), *Doing qualitative analysis in psychology* (pp. 245–272). London: Taylor & Francis.

Pryzwansky, W. B. (1986). Indirect service delivery: Considerations for future research in consultation. *School Psychology Review, 15,* 479–488.

Pryzwansky, W. B., & Noblit, G. W. (1990). Understanding and improving consultation practice: The qualitative case study approach. *Journal of Educational and Psychological Consultation, 1,* 293–307.

Rosenfield, S. (1991). The relationship variable in behavioral consultation. *Journal of Behavioral Education, 1,* 329–336.

Sandoval, J. (1996). Constructivism, consultee-centered consultation, and conceptual change. *Journal of Educational and Psychological Consultation, 7,* 89–97.

Sandoval, J. (1999). Evaluation issues and strategies in consultee-centered consultation. In I. Hylander & G. Guvå (Eds.), *Explorations in process in practice, 101–104.* (Seminar proceedings). Stockholm: 2nd International Seminar on Consultee-Centered Consultation.

Sandoval, J., & Lambert, N. (1987). Evaluating school psychologists and school psychological services. In B. A. Edelstein and E. S. Berler (Eds.), *Evaluation and accountability in clinical training* (pp. 151–182). New York: Plenum Press.

Starrin, B., Larsson, G., Dahlgren L., & Styrborn, S. (1991). *Från upptäckt till presentation. Om kvalitativ metod och teorigenerering på empirisk grund* [From discovery to presentation. About qualitative method and theory generation on empirical ground]. Lund: Studentlitteratur.

Stern, D. (1985). *The interpersonal world of the infant.* New York: Basic Books.

Stern, P. N. (1980). Grounded theory methodology: Its uses and processes. *Image, 12,* 20–23.

Stern, P. N. (1994). Eroding grounded theory. In J. Morse (Ed.), *Critical issues in qualitative research* (pp. 212–223). Thousand Oaks, CA: Sage.

Strauss, A. (1987). *Qualitative analysis for social scientist.* New York: Cambridge University Press.

Strauss, A., & Corbin, J. (1990). *Basics of qualitative research: Grounded Theory procedures and techniques.* Newbury Park, CA: Sage.

Thörn, S. (1999). Listen to the contradictory and emphasize the ambiguous. On change and development. In I. Hylander & G. Guvå (Eds.), *Explorations in process in practice, 111–114.* (Seminar proceedings). Stockholm: 2nd International Seminar on Consultee-Centered Consultation.

Vygotsky, L. S. (1970). *Thought and language.* Cambridge, MA: MIT Press

Vygotsky, L. S. (1978). *Mind in society: The development of higher psychological processes.* Cambridge, MA: Harvard University Press.

Winnicott, D. (1971). *Playing and reality.* NewYork: Basic books

Wiström, C. (1990). Konsultation i skolan. Teori och metodik under 2 decennier. *Psykologtidningen, 20.*

Wiström, C. (1990). Konsultation i skolam. Teori och metodik under 2 decennier [Consultation in schools. Theory and methods during 2 decades]. *Psykologtidningen, 20,* 4–9.

Wiström, C., Hanson, M,. Qvarnström, G., & Westerlund, S. (1995). *Psykologisk konsultation i pedagogisk verksamhet. Analys och utvärdering av konsultationsarbete i banomsorg och skola* [Psychological consultation in educational settings. Analyses and assessments of consultation to child care and schools]. Östersund, Sweden: Östersunds kommun, Konsult & Service, Pedagogica.

Ingrid Hylander is an Assistant Professor of Psychology at Linköping University in Sweden. She has extensive experience as a consulting psychologist to the Swedish childcare system and schools. She and colleagues have developed applications of consultee-centered consultation to serve childcare workers. Her research interests are in consultation processes, group psychology, and child development, with a special interest in qualitative research methodology.

JOURNAL OF EDUCATIONAL AND PSYCHOLOGICAL CONSULTATION, *14*(3&4), 281–301

Mediation of Consultee's Conceptual Development in New Teacher Groups: Using Questions to Improve Coherency

Linda Webster
University of the Pacific

Steven E. Knotek
University of North Carolina at Chapel Hill

Leslie M. Babinski
Bucknell University

Dwight L. Rogers
University of North Carolina at Chapel Hill

Mary M. Barnett
Alogonquin Regional High School, Northboro, MA

This qualitative study applied methods used in discourse analysis to investigate how a consultant's questioning supported the goal of group consultation to empower beginning teachers to become effective problem solvers in their work environment. The focus of the study was on the process of questioning and communicative coherency as the group evolved over the course of the school year. The participants in this study were 7 White elementary school teachers in their first year of teaching. There were 12 sessions held over an 8-month period. The investigators found evidence of a parallel process be-

Correspondence should be addressed to Linda Webster, University of the Pacific, 3601 Pacific Avenue, Stockton, CA 95211. E-mail: lwebster@uop.edu

tween the coordinate consultation process and coherency in consultative discourse, such that as the coordinate process developed and improved, so did the coherency of group discourse. Implications for practice, training, and future research are discussed.

The first years of teaching are a critical period in the development of new teachers' ability to meet the complex educational and social needs of their students (Danielson, 1999; Garcia & Harris, 1998). During this time of entry into the profession, novice teachers begin the tremendous task of attempting to meet ever more stringent teaching objectives in classes with children from an ever more socially and ethnically diverse student body. Beginning teachers often lack the sophistication and professional experience necessary to both adequately conceptualize the intricate issues inherent in such challenging teaching environments and to implement the multifaceted interactions required. Around the United States, school districts have begun to recognize these problems associated with inadequate new teacher induction and have begun implementing various forms of mentoring programs.

QUESTIONING

Group consultation for new teachers holds promise as a means for new teachers to problem-solve and find support for the challenges of their first year of teaching while continuing to build their skills and balance multiple tasks (Babinski & Rogers, 1998). A consultant can play a key role by facilitating group processes and employing skillful and thoughtful questioning to generate a more accurate and contextualized representation of the teachers' problems. Communication skills in general, and questioning skills in particular, are at the heart of the consultative process (Erchul, 1993; Safran, 1991). Group consultation with multiple consultees may be especially reliant on the successful use of questioning to manage a coordinate and constructive consultative process. Coordinate processes are described by Caplan and Caplan (1993) as the responsive, iterative interactions between consultant and consultee that characterize a social dimension of consultation. In contrast, constructive processes (Sandoval, 2003; Marshall, 1992) describe a cognitive dimension in consultation that is associated with a shift in the consultee's point of view on the work problem. Ivey, Pedersen, and Ivey (2001) classify questioning as a key leadership skill necessary to successfully facilitate problem-solving groups. Through thoughtful questioning, it is expected that a more accurate representation of the problem—one with fewer distortions—will result in the ability to deal more directly with the dilemma.

The questioning process has long been considered to be one of the key tenants of the consultee-centered process (Caplan & Caplan, 1993). However, we know very little about how the questioning process actually plays out in the consultative dynamic of a New Teacher Group (NTG). What kinds of consultant's questions encourage orderly reflection? Within a consultation group, how does the consultant manage the process of questioning with consultees who are at developmentally different levels? What does the discourse look like in the group as the questioning promotes reflection and the consideration of multiple perspectives?

In keeping with Sandoval's (1996, this issue) model of conceptual change in consultation, it is our premise that the consultant facilitates the process by asking questions designed to illuminate the consultation dilemma. The consultant attempts to understand the consultee's theory of the nature of the problem, and attempts to make a nonjudgmental assessment of the defensive processes that may be distorting the true nature of the problem (and thus clouding potential solutions). Group consultation can facilitate this process by offering multiple perspectives and thus allowing the consultee to develop a more coherent, flexible, and contextualized version of the problem. Ideally, one goal of the consultation experience would be that the consultee would begin to develop metarepresentational processes that allow him or her to be able to reflect on the validity, nature, and source of their dilemma.

By examining the discourse in the NTGs, this study investigates how consultant's questioning supported the goal of group consultation to empower the teachers to become effective problem solvers in their work environment. To that end, this article focuses on the process of questioning and communicative coherency as the group evolved over the course of the school year.

MENTAL REPRESENTATIONS

Bowlby (1973, 1980) originally hypothesized the existence of a "mental representation" of relationships that guided attachment behavior, feeling, and thought. Researchers have since found that mental representations can be reliably measured through an analysis of an individual's narrative regarding their attachment relationship with their parents (Hesse, 1999). Furthermore, research has shown that narrative methods can be used to assess the mental representations that parents hold for their relationship with their children (Bretherton, Biringin, & Ridgeway, 1991), and the mental representations that teachers hold for their students (Stulman & Pianta, 2002). The coherency of the mental representation of the consultee with regards to the conceptualization of a consultation problem is deemed to be a critical component of effective consultee-centered consultation. Distortions, defensive processes, miscommunications, inadequate information, and premature definitions of problems can all contribute to an impaired coherency of the consultation problem. As the consultation progresses, the conceptualization of the problem is co-constructed by the parties involved (Sandoval, 1996), with the goal being a well-developed and contextualized understanding of the problem that is relatively free of distortions and defenses, and flexibly integrates both positive and negative aspects of the situation.

Teachers' mental representations are thought to be influenced by a number of factors, including their representational models of relationships between teachers and children in general, their feelings and beliefs about teaching in general, and their goals with a specific child at a specific time (Pianta, 1999). Pianta and colleagues' research on teachers' narratives indicates that teachers' mental representations of their relationships with their students are organized by a set of information processing rules that regulate information and affect in a consistent and predictable manner (Stuhlman & Pianta, 2002). This is consistent with the research literature on parents' mental representations of their care-giving relationships with their children (George & Solomon, 1996). Furthermore, Stuhlman and Pianta (2002) have found that teachers' internal working models, or mental "blueprints" of their relationship with a specific child, can be examined in their narratives about that child. This finding suggests that a teacher's discourse during consultation can not only be analyzed, but can provide a window into the modification of that mental representation. We have thus extended this concept to investigate the coherency of the narrative as a method to examine the effectiveness of group consultation with new teachers.

COHERENCY

Coherency, as defined in this study, is a quality of speaking that is logically connected, internally consistent, relevant to the topic under discussion, and collaborative with the other members of the group. For the purpose of this study, our working definition of coherency was loosely based upon Grice's (1975) four maxims of discourse coherency: quality, quantity, relation, and manner (especially the maximum of quality in conversation). The definition was also influenced by Main's (1991), George and Solomon's (1996), and George, West, and Pettem's (1997) conceptualizations of Bowlby's defensive processes (1980). The goal of the study was to investigate the coherency of the NTG discourse as a function of consultant questioning, and later in the year, consultee questioning.

Grice's (1975) maxim of quality requires that the speaker be truthful, or accurate, and to have supportive evidence for their position, or, in this case, their interpretation of the consultation dilemma. The maxim of quantity requires the speaker to give enough information such that the dilemma is readily apparent to the group members, but not so much information that the listeners become lost in the details or the speaker begins repeating themselves in a seeming effort to convince others of their viewpoint without really adding additional, pertinent information. The maxim of relation refers to the relevancy of the discourse turn. This maxim requires that the speaker stay on topic as opposed to jumping from topic to topic, or discussing issues that have no bearing on the dilemma under consideration. Finally, the maxim of manner requires the speaker to be clear and orderly in their speech. Violations of these maxims may be licensed whenever the speaker demonstrates a conscious awareness that they are being incoherent. For example, if the speaker begins a lengthy passage by prefacing it with, "It's a long story," this gives the speaker permission to be lengthy. If the speaker admits that they may sound confusing because they are themselves confused, this gives license to a reduction in quality. It is thought that the ability to reflect on one's knowledge and acknowledge incoherencies should lead to increased coherency (Main, 1991), and reflect a flexible mental representation of the consultation dilemma.

A discourse turn is considered coherent if it addresses a topic at hand and is clear, concise, and consistent. A discourse turn is considered incoherent when defensive thinking processes cause the mental representation (and thus the discourse) to become distorted and disorganized, and limit the recognition and exploration of options. The consultant (and other group members) can aid in the development of a more accurate and coherent mental representation by asking questions that illuminate inconsistencies and inaccuracies in such a way that the consultee can begin to reflect upon their experience and mental representation, and reorganize it so that it is more contextualized and coherent.

THE STUDY

This study builds upon prior research (Babinski & Rogers, 1998; Knotek, Babinski, & Rogers, 2002) to further examine the process of NTGs as a form of consultee-centered consultation. While we have identified that NTGs support changes in consultees' understanding of students, the specific consultative processes surrounding these changes have not been studied. In this investigation, we examine how one core consultative process, question-posing (Caplan & Caplan, 1993), is used in a NTG. Specifically, we investigated when questions were used during the process, who used questions and to what purpose, and finally, how question posing did or did not support the consultative process.

METHOD

Participants

The participants in this study were seven White elementary school teachers in their first year of teaching. Five of the participants were women and two were men; all were in their early to mid-20s. They taught Grade 2 through 5 in seven different schools in suburban and rural communities. The teachers were invited to participate in the NTG during their orientation programs in their districts. The teachers agreed to meet every other week throughout the school year to discuss their issues and concerns with a consultant, or group facilitator. The consultant, Barnett, was a graduate student in a school psychology program at a local university who received training and supervision in consultation and research from university faculty. Prior to the study the consultant had completed four courses, with supervised practica, in consultation and intervention.

Procedure

A micro-ethnographic approach, which is an in-depth study of a small number of individuals in a naturalistic setting, was used to examine teachers' discussions within a consultation group in the 1997 to 1998 school year (Bogdan & Biklen, 1992; Erickson, 1986; Fetterman, 1989). This approach is ideally suited for the study of the interpersonal discourse interactions among group members (Rogers & Babinski, 2002). The main unit of study, or *focal event*, was defined as a collaborative discussion in which teachers and a consultant engaged in a problem-solving process about issues of concern.

There were 12, 1½ hr group consultation sessions over an 8-month period. A problem-solving format was used in the group to provide a framework for the discussions (Knotek et al., 2002). Although the consultant provided the structure, the teachers were free to introduce any topics of concern to them. The types of topics discussed in NTG and the teachers' perceptions of NTG have been reported elsewhere (Babinski & Rogers, 1998; Rogers & Babinski, 2002).

Qualitative data for this study was gathered by the use of five main types of collection procedures: (a) participant-observation by the consultant, (b) audio-recording and transcription of the sessions, (c) field notes written by the consultant after the sessions, (d) post-group reflections written by the consultant and participants, and (e) end-of-the-year interviews with each member of the group that were recorded and transcribed. The end-of-the-year interviews were conducted for the purpose of ongoing research and evaluation. These individual interviews were .5 to 1 hr in length and covered questions such as the participant's perceptions of the process and the efficacy of the group in supporting his or her professional development. These data sources formed the basis for initial process notes.

Data Analysis

The data analysis was aimed at both describing and understanding how the consultation process within a NTG supported consultees' development. The first step in the analysis was to collect data and examine them for evidence of reoccurring topics within and across groups and individuals. After the initial search for related topics, Grice's (1975) four maxims of discourse coherency (i.e., quality, quantity, relevance, and manner) were adopted and used in the first round of coding the data for both the interviews and the audio-taped sessions. In order to provide a means to discretely observe developmental trends within the group, six sessions were chosen for microanalysis. Two sessions each were taken from the beginning, middle, and end of the year. It was reasoned that these time frames would show sufficient distinctions in coherency in order for patterns and trends in the data to be analyzed. While data from the entire year were used to identify the initial topics, these six sessions were minutely scrutinized to describe the actual communicative process of questioning within the consultation. Data were coded by Webster and Knotek. Webster received extensive training on multiple occasions on discourse-analysis methods utilized in attachment narratives and had achieved reliability in coding on over 80 cases in related measures. This coding schema was adapted for usage in this study, and Knotek was trained by Webster. Discrepancies in coding were handled via conferencing.

Coherency.   All of the data sources, but primarily the transcripts, were coded on a 3-point coherency scale in which participants' conceptualization of the consultation problem were rated from 0 (*low*) to 1 (*moderate*) to 2 (*high*). Interactions that were preceded or followed by the consultant's questions were especially focused upon (see Table 1) .

Transcripts of the interviews, the field notes, and documents were tagged, matched, and then integrated according to coherency scores and patterns. The integrated data were then imported into the QSRN6 qualitative data management software program along hierarchically indexed nodes of participant role, individual, and session. Next, these categories were coded according to constructive processes (Marshall, 1992) and coordinate processes (Caplan & Caplan, 1993).

Constructive process.   The *constructive process* is defined as a consultant's support of a consultee's acquisition of a new perspective on the work problem. This process occurs through the use of appropriate communication strategies to assist the consultee in the restructuring of prior knowledge or the construction of new understandings. Strategies used to support a constructive process include pinpointing critical information and responding to the consultee's content. Codes for this process were based on Marshall's (1992) descriptions (see Table 1).

Coordinate process.   Based upon Caplan and Caplan (1993), this process describes the reciprocal, communicative give-and-take between consultant and consultee. When consultation is in a coordinate state both participants are active and respond to and inform the other (see Table 1). The codes were based upon the main descriptors used in Caplan's discussion of the coordinate process (1993, pp. 356–359).

Finally, the data were then searched for themes and patterns and re-collated along three themed nodes (see Table 1). This process produced three reoccurring themes that spanned sessions and individuals (a) use of question-posing to promote a coordinate relationship, (b) teachers' use of questions, and (c) questioning to mediate coherency.

RESULTS AND DISCUSSION

Question-Posing to Promote a Coordinate Relationship

Joining or bridging questions were built into the consultative process of the NTG through two embedded processes called *updates* and *brags and drags*. At some point during each session the consultant would create a

TABLE 1

Summary of Coding Categories

Category	Description
Coherency	
Low (0)	Marked incoherence of mind with regard to problem. Multiple contradictions between the abstract description or conceptualization of the problem and specific evidence supplied by the consultee to support their conceptualization. Little reciprocal engagement with consultee.
Moderate (1)	Moderate coherency in regards to the consultation problem. Problem outlined with minimal description. No contradictions between conceptualization and evidence.
High (2)	Problem is presented in consistent, coherent terms. Consultee and consultant engage in reciprocal examination of multiple perspectives.
Constructive (Con)	Support construction of new point of view through questioning and challenging. Communication congruent with consultee's conceptions and ideas.
Content (c)	(a) Consultant listens to breadth of consultee's content, selectively pinpoints information.
	(b) Use/respond to consultee's content/viewpoint.
	(c) Consultant's alternative view made available to the consultee.
Process (p)	(a) Consultee chooses from what is discussed.
	(b) Consultant challenges/guides consultee through clarification, expanding, and taking alternative point of view.
Coordinate (Coo)	Reciprocal, coordinated give and take. Both active communicants.
Consultant (ct)	(a) Respect: non-evaluative questions and responses.
	(b) Non hierarchical: consultee free to accept or reject input, mutual constructions and clarifications.
	(c) Foster independence: Provides think-time, does not unnecessarily rescue, encourages consultee's active problem solving.
	(d) Questions match consultee's stated needs.
Consultee (ce)	(a) Educates consultant about work setting.
	(b) Describes complications of work role with regard to client.
	(c) Reciprocal communication to help consultant pinpoint difficulties, understand the problem.
	(d) Active dependent: Engages consultant to think through issues, construct new understandings.

(Continued)

289

TABLE 1 (*Continued*)

Category	Description
Themed nodes	
Question posing to promote a coordinate relationship	Patterns of high to moderate coherency associated with consultant's use of questions in regards to consultee's prior content (Coding ex: 2 Coo ct d).
Teacher's use of questions	Teacher's parallel assumption of role of questioner. Teachers' responses coded as constructive and/or coordinate process that had characteristics associated with the role of consultant (Coding ex: Teacher-1 Con p b).
Questioning to mediate coherency	Consultant's use of low or medium/high coherency questioning to inhibit/support the process of reflection, consideration of alternate view points, while building upon consultee's prior knowledge (Coding ex: 0 –Coo ct b).

Note. Coherency codes based on Grice (1975). Constructive process codes based on Marshall (1992). Coordinate process codes based on Caplan and Caplan (1993).

connection between the group and the teachers' work settings, and also link the current and prior sessions by asking the questions, "Does anyone have any brags or drags to share?" and "Are there any updates?" (Rogers & Babinski, 2002).

The brags and drags, a time set aside to discuss the prior week's events, were embedded in the weekly process to give the teachers the overt opportunity to discuss experiences that they found to be meaningful. While the content varied weekly and by participant, these questions were part of a formal process in which the consultees' knowledge and experiences were the center points of the groups' existence. The update questions frequently occurred at the beginning of each meeting and served the dual effect of establishing temporal contiguity between the conversations in each session, and perhaps most importantly, of explicitly valuing the teachers' concerns and perspectives.

Updates.   Updates also served the purpose of increasing the relevancy of the discourse and established a collaborative relationship. The following conversation illustrates how the consultant's question-posing helped establish the quality of the relationship (NTG meeting). The consultant, Mary, is referred to in the dialogue quotations as C/Mary.

> C/Mary: I also wanted to get started. Does anybody have anything that they want to revisit from last time? The only thing that I remember was Tina's situation and Tina's not here. I don't know if Sam, if you felt like you needed to talk any more about what you did with your students as far as having them work hard on activities and to bring their grade up, do you have anything to add to that or not?
>
> Sam: My students have been great the past couple of weeks.
>
> C/Mary: What did you do? Did you say something to them about it?
>
> Sam: I've been doing a couple of follow-up activities. Like one of our counselors came in and talked about respect. I think I made it serious to my kids to behave. She was asking them about somebody they respect and why. My kids were getting too specific and weren't giving very good details, let's say, "I respect Michael Jordan because he makes a lot of money." And so, she was running lessons, so I wasn't going to say anything. I just took notes,

notes, notes of what the kids were saying. So we went back and talked about more in depth the reason...

C/Mary: And you feel that things are better?

Sam: Yeah. That whole test was just a fluke. It's because I did say, "This doesn't count, this isn't worth anything. Just do your best and try the hardest."

In this interaction the consultant's questions were consultee-focused in that they served to put the emphasis of the conversation on the consultee's perspective: "...they [*you*] want to revisit?" "Do *you* have anything to add?" "What did *you* do?" "Did *you* say...?" "Are *you* feeling that things are better?" "Do *you* still feel that way?" These questions also promoted an iterative process within the consultation, in that the consultee played an integral part in the conversation's give-and-take, and the consultee supported the consultant's understanding of the work problem. Questions were useful in not only gathering information, they also served to establish the coordinate relationship between the consultant and the consultee.

Brags and drags.   During brags and drags the focus on relevancy was also linked to an increase in the coherency of the group. Within these conversations it was the consultant's task to ask nonevaluative questions and then listen. The following remarks about this aspect of the NTG process come from three of the teachers' year-end interviews.

[The NTG was] good support. I looked forward to talking. Someone told me it was a, was a waste of time, and I said, "No, it really helps." (Austin)

[NTG] was set up so you personally could reflect on something you have been doing well. You just don't do that in staff meetings. ... and this sense of appreciation from people, and being able to reflect on a problem and to have people who want to take it apart or at least listen to it. (Sarah)

[I] felt totally comfortable [to discuss] any situation [brag or drag] that I had. [I] felt I would be respected and my problems not blown off. (Sabrina)

The brags and drags fostered a consultee-centered environment in the NTG because they provided the consultant an opportunity to respectfully listen to the perspective and values of the teachers. In turn, as the teachers educated the consultant about the work issue they were able to reflect on their own understandings of the problem. The comments from the teachers above suggest a willingness to engage in the self-reflection process and to explore his or her internal working hypothesis of the consultation problem.

Teachers Use of Questions

Question-posing plays a fundamental role in the facilitation of the consultation process because it is through judicious questioning that consultants help consultees clarify their current understandings of the work problem and widen their focus to include new possibilities, through which consultants themselves actively become coparticipants in the problem-solving process (Caplan, 1970).

Over the course of this NTG the pattern of question-posing evolved as the group progressed (see Table 2). Initially, the consultant asked the overwhelming majority of the questions in relation to the teachers (19 consultant questions vs. 4 teacher questions). However, as the year progressed the proportion of questions posed by the teachers grew, and by the end of the year there was a balance in the overall total of questions posed (109 consultant questions vs. 117 teacher questions). This shift in questioning marks a change in the overall process of the consultation. At year's end, both the teachers and the consultant were jointly active in facilitating understandings of the various work problems. This movement towards a balance in the act of questioning may be construed as one indication that the consultation was increasingly becoming a coordinate process in that the teachers were becoming more independent and the social roles less hierarchical. Question-posing in and of itself, though, does not increase the effec-

TABLE 2
Frequency of Questions Posed by the Consultant (Ct) and Teachers

Session Date	Low Coherence		High Coherence		Total	
	Ct	Teachers	Ct	Teachers	Ct	Teachers
10/8	6	1	13	3	19	4
10/22	8	3	18	7	26	10
12/3	1	7	10	36	11	43
1/14	0	2	13	20	13	23
2/11	0	0	16	25	16	25
3/4	1	0	23	13	23	13
Total	16	13	93	104	109	117

Note.   Low Coherency = Score < 1, High Coherence = Score ≥ 1.

tiveness of the consultation; the characteristics of the questions that were asked must also be considered.

In addition to changes in the simple frequency of questions, there was also development in the quality of the questions that were posed. Although overall low-coherency questions were used less frequently than high-coherency questions, as the year progressed the proportion of high-coherency to low-coherency questions increased for both the consultant and the consultees (see Table 1).

The low-coherency questions tended to have the aim of advice-giving that created a push for a premature solution. The following three examples from the first session illustrate this inclination.

> Teacher: I feel like I'm a babysitter and not a teacher. It's making sure their homework gets done and sitting next to them. And, I'm not like this is a waste of time, but I don't have an assistant to do [it].
> Consultant: Have you talked to your administrators?
> Teacher: (Shares a room with another teacher) I think she sensed that I was frustrated. I haven't said anything out loud…
> Consultant: Do you think she'd be willing to switch sides?
> Teacher: The problem is that she has all these meetings with the volunteers and she does it in her room.
> Teacher 2: Do you think if you suggested…do you think she would really be into listening to you say that?

In each of these examples the consultation process was short-circuited because the consultees' understanding of the issues went unexplored and the process moved forward almost immediately to advice-giving. This form of questioning impeded the consultee's construction of a new perspective on the work problem.

While low coherence was a quality often found in questions in the early sessions, as the year progressed low-coherence questions became infrequent, and the overall majority of the questions became increasingly more coherent (see Table 1). The following exchange, which occurred during one of the last meetings, illustrates this trend. The consultant has just asked a question and set the tone for the group to collaboratively question Tom.

> Tom: He's real smart [but] doesn't do any of his work [and] when he does do it he does it for like 10 seconds and gets about 80% of it right. [This occurs] without, even

> putting the thought into it. So, I really hope he gets into that…
>
> Sabrina: Have you already gone through the whole referral process?
>
> Tom: … Is all I had to do was check off his strong points on a permission slip, send a permission slip, and he's being tested Monday.
>
> Sabrina: Wow, what does that mean for you? Will he be taken out of class for 30 minutes a day every day or once a week?

In this brief exchange Sabrina asks questions that serve to further Tom's exploration of his work problem. The initial question focuses on pinpointing critical information necessary to understand Tom's viewpoint. Tom then provides a coordinate response in which he helps his collaborator understand specifics of the issue. Sabrina next follows with a question in which she guides Tom to expand his view of the issue. This exchange demonstrates how the NTG developed a collaborative process in which the teachers themselves used questioning to facilitate a peer's problem-solving.

Questioning to Mediate Coherency

The aim of the NTG is to support new teachers' ability to engage in effective problem-solving. This goal is accomplished through the process of consultation in the course of which the consultant uses questions and dialogue to (a) engage teachers in reflection, (b) support their consideration of alternative views, and (c) guide their development of more complete understandings. Conversations are the coin of the realm in consultation—they are the medium through which the consultant engages the consultee in an examination of the work problem. Therefore, it is critical that the conversations effectively engage all individuals and allow for clarity in the expression and mutual understanding of the participants' meanings. Grice (1975) describes this quality of speaking as coherency.

Conversations that are coherent (Grice, 1975) are collaborative, consistent, connected, and relevant. Applied to consultation, this means that the quality of the conversations directly affects (a) the coordinate give-and-take between the consultant and the consultees, and (b) the usefulness of questions to respectfully challenge and guide the consultee. Over the course of this NTG there were both positive and negative examples of how the quality of coherency affected the consultation process.

Negative effect of low coherency. Although question-posing could be used to sharpen and contextualize the conversation, there were times when premature question-posing had the effect of working against the constructive and coordinate processes in the consultation. Especially in the early sessions, the group members had a tendency to present their own constructions of a person's issue, often in the service of advice-giving, before trying to fully understand that person's perception of the problem. The following interchange between Tom, who has presented a problem, and Sarah, who is asking questions, illustrates this theme.

> Tom: I think something was, I think the fact that the notes aren't coming now is somehow related to the conference. But I don't know exactly, because we didn't discuss it.
> Sarah: Do you think that the mom did see something to gripe about? And now that she has this gripe with the assistant, that's her focus now instead of ... Do you think that mom is just like a little, you know, loopy?
> Tom: Well, historically, she has been known to be sort of loopy.
> Sarah: So do you think that this might be her one, this is her focus now?
> Tom: Maybe, but either that or I think that she just needed to get in there and talk to me, and just having that contact, I mean, because of one or two times she's come into the room and basically said, "Blah, blah, blah." And I've in turn said, "Blah."

At the beginning of this interaction Tom's comments are somewhat vague as he is first trying to make sense of the problem. Sarah's question, "Do you think mom is loopy?" is not predicated upon anything that Tom has just said, and represents her own conjecture or mental representation about the situation. In response to this question Tom takes Sarah's lead and tries to build off of Sarah's construction of the problem. At that point the process is not coordinate for the consultee, and Tom spends the next few sentences trying to sort out his ideas from Sarah's ideas. The process has reached a point in which the give-and-take is no longer centered on the consultee's conceptions, and the consultee must actively struggle to reject a member's input.

Premature question-posing, coupled with opinion giving, was the phenomenon most associated with low coherency in this NTG. While it occurred across the year, the majority of these questions were asked during the first sessions (see Table 1).

Positive effect of high coherency.   The most coherent conversations in the NTG were characterized by the presence of questions that promoted co-ordinate interactions and facilitated a constructive problem-solving pro-cess. The following is an example of a discussion that was characterized by high coherency.

It is a January afternoon and the group is meeting for the first time in the new year. The members have spent the initial part of the session discussing their vacations and the effects of time off on both teachers and students. Mary, the consultant, helps the group focus by asking a consultee-focused question.

> C/Mary: Well who's having a problem in their classroom that they want to talk about?

After Mary asks this embedded, joining question, Tom responds by provid-ing the consultant with a description of a work problem.

> Tom: I've got a new boy in my classroom. This is my second new boy. I had one new boy who came and left. I didn't think that he was going to last. He came from Markham and his mother moved quickly, he left under duress so I didn't think that he would be around that long.

While Tom has responded to Mary's question, the description needs to be much fuller before they can begin to problem-solve. In the next sequence of interactions Tom and Mary engage in a coordinated exchange in which they build up the representation of the problem.

> C/Mary: How long was he there?
> Tom: He was there, at the shelter? How long was he here in my classroom?
> C/Mary: How long was he there in your classroom?

Tom responds to this series of questions by presenting a lengthy descrip-tion of the student within the context of his classroom. The consultant then asks some questions that serve to broaden Tom's view of the stu-dent's situation.

> C/Mary: Have you talked to his parents?
> Tom: No, even when I went out and met his mother she was-n't very talkative and no I haven't called her yet.

C/Mary: How long has he been here for?

Tom: He has been here for a week. This will be his second week. I was going to try and work with him myself and then I'm going to give him a couple of weeks to adjust because this is a big adjustment in the middle of the year going into a small classroom.

In this last exchange Tom begins to present his thinking about an important aspect of the problem, "a big adjustment." The conversation has been set up as a series of questions that prompt give-and-take responses between the consultant and the consultee. Each of them assumes a particular role in the formulation and posing of the questions; they are participating in a consultee-centered conversation. At this point another teacher joins in and begins to ask questions that promote Tom's construction of a new view of the problem. The conversation remains consultee-focused and it ends when Tom indicates that he is ready to move on to another topic.

CONCLUSION

This investigation has attempted to merge theory and research on consultee-centered case consultation with theory and research on mental representations of relationships. The investigators found evidence of a parallel process between the coordinate consultation process and coherency in consultative discourse, such that as the coordinate process developed and improved, so did the coherency of group discourse. Conversely, when the coordinate process stumbled or failed, so did the coherency. The coordinate process also appears to serve a positive function in the development of reflection in group members. Both of these findings have implications for understanding and improving consultee-centered case consultation.

First, it suggests that one of the mechanisms of improving reflection and coherency resides in the coordinate process. This has implications for the training of school consultants, as it provides support for the position that consultation cannot be reduced to a set of prescribed interactions or interventions, and must be co-constructed by the consultant and the consultee (Sandoval, this issue). To do this effectively, the consultant must be guided by the theory of consultation as well as child development to formulate questions that serve as a scaffold for the consultee to bridge their understandings of children and learning with their mental representation of the particular problem. In addition, these preliminary findings suggest it is important that the consultant possess the disposition to resist premature problem-solving and advice-giving regardless of how compelling it is. This investigation can serve as a demonstration to nascent consultants that premature problem-solving and advice-giving actually contributes to incoherency.

Second, the findings of this investigation provide further support to the notion that the focus should be on the narrative as the window into understanding the mental representations of the consultee. This is consistent with research that has been conducted on parent–child relationships (George & Solomon, 1996) and teacher–child relationships (Stuhlman & Pianta, 2002), which indicates that mental representations as measured by narratives can be reliably identified and are directly related to behavioral interactions between the adult and child. Mental representations, captured in discourse, reflect patterns in thoughts, interpretations, and expectations that influence behavior in relationships. Consultant questions that are designed to gently and respectfully challenge the consultee's mental representation were found in this study to improve coherence. Questions that did not assume unstated knowledge, but rather focused on increasing the contextualization of the mental representation, were found to improve overall coherence in teacher's narratives across discussions and across students discussed. This is an important theoretical consideration, since it implies that teachers' narratives are more a function of their internal mental representations about children and teaching in general, as opposed to specific interactions between a given teacher and a particular child.

Finally, the results of this study bolster the contention that consultee-centered consultation is a constructive process that entails a joint development of a new conceptualization of the work problem (Knotek & Sandoval, 2003; Sandoval, 2003). Effective questioning supports consultees acquisition of new ways to conceptualize and approach work-related dilemmas.

Limitations

Several methodological limitations constrain the results of the study. The addition of an external auditor would have enhanced the neutrality and the objectivity of the data analysis. Because of time and logistical constraints, member checking was not used and this limitation impacts the internal validity of the findings. Additionally, the study of a larger sample of groups would better support both the applicability and credibility of the findings. Finally, the decision to focus the analysis on 6 sessions instead of all 12 may have affected the overall results.

Future Research

This preliminary study leaves many important variables unaccounted for and many questions unanswered. Future research should investigate how variables, such as consultant's experience, consultee's verbal engagement, and variations in student population, impact the mediation of consultee's conceptual development. Ultimately, it would also be important for future research to add a classroom observation component to determine whether a change in the coherency of the mental representation translates into improved interactions in the classroom.

REFERENCES

Babinski, L. M., & Rogers, D. L. (1998). Supporting new teachers through consultee-centered group consultation. *Journal of Educational and Psychological Consultation, 9*, 285–308.

Bogdan, R., & Biklen, S. (1992). *Qualitative research for education: An introduction to theory and methods.* Needham Heights, MA: Allyn & Bacon.

Bowlby, J. (1973). *Attachment and loss* (Vol. 2., Separation). New York: Basic Books.

Bowlby, J. (1980). *Attachment and loss* (Vol. 3,. Loss). New York: Basic Books.

Bowlby, J. (1982). *Attachment and loss* (Vol. 1., Attachment). New York: Basic Books.

Bretherton, I., Biringen, Z., & Ridgeway, D. (1991). The parental side of attachment. In K. Pillemer & K. McCartney (Eds.), *Parent child relations throughout life.* (pp. 1–24). Hillsdale, NJ: Lawrence Erlbaum Associates, Inc.

Caplan, G. (1970). *Theory and practice of mental health consultation.* New York: Basic Books.

Caplan, G., & Caplan, R. B. (1993). *Mental health consultation and collaboration.* San Francisco: Jossey-Bass.

Danielson, C. (1999). Mentoring beginning teachers: The case for mentoring. *Teaching and Change, 6*, 251–257.

Erchul, W. P. (1993). Selected interpersonal perspectives in consultation research. *School Psychology Quarterly, 8*, 38–49.

Erickson, F. (1986). Qualitative methods in research on teaching. In M. C. Wittrock (Ed.), *Handbook of Research on Teaching* (3rd ed., pp. 119–161). New York: Macmillian.

Fetterman, D. M. (1989). *Ethnography step by step.* Newbury Park, CA: Sage.

Garcia, E. E., & Harris, J. R. (1998). Teachers developing teachers: A new resource for the challenge ahead. *Teacher Education Quarterly, 25*, 134–138.

George, C., & Solomon, J. (1996). Representational models of relationships: Links between care giving and attachment. *Infant Mental Health Journal, 17*, 198–216.

George, C., West, M., & Pettem, O. (1997). *The Adult Attachment Projective.* Unpublished attachment measure and coding manual. Mills College, Oakland, CA.

Grice, H. P. (1975). Logic and conversation. In P. Cole & J. L. Moran (Eds.), *Syntax and semantics III: Speech acts* (pp. 41–58). New York: Academic.

Hesse, E. (1999). The Adult Attachment Interview: Historical and current perspectives. In J. Cassidy & P. R. Shaver (Eds.), *Handbook of attachment* (pp. 395–433). New York: Guilford.

Ivey, A. E., Pedersen, P. B., & Ivey, M. B. (2001). *Intentional group counseling: A micro skills approach.* Belmont, CA: Wadsworth.

Knotek, S. E., Babinski, L. M., & Rogers, D. L. (2002). Consultation in new teacher groups: Facilitating collaboration among new teachers. *California School Psychologist, 7*, 39–50.

Main, M. (1991). Metacognitive knowledge, metacognitive monitoring, and singular (coherent) vs. multiple (incoherent) model of attachment. In C. M. Parkes, J. Stevenson-Hinde, & P. Harris (Eds.), *Attachment across the life-cycle* (pp. 127–159). London: Routledge.

Marshall, H. M. (1992, April). *Reconceptualizing learning for restructured schools.* Paper presented at the annual meeting of the American Educational Research Association, San Francisco, CA.

Pianta, R. C. (1999). *Enhancing relationships between children and teachers.* Washington, DC: American Psychological Association.

Rogers, D. L., & Babinski, L. M. (2002). *From isolation to conversation: Supporting new teachers' development.* Albany, NY: State University of New York Press.

Safran, S. P. (1991). The communication process and school-based consultation: What does the research say? *Journal of Educational and Psychological Consultation, 8*, 93–100.

Sandoval, J. (1996). Constructivism, consultee-centered consultation and conceptual change. *Journal of Educational and Psychological Consultation, 7*, 89–97.

Stuhlman, M. W., & Pianta, R. C. (2002). Teachers' narratives about their relationships with children: Associations with behavior in classrooms. *School Psychology Review, 31*, 148–163.

Linda Webster is an Associate Professor in the school psychology program at the University of the Pacific in Stockton, CA. Her research interests lie in the study of mental representations of relationships and their influence on behavior in children, teachers, and parents.

Steven E. Knotek is an Assistant Professor of School Psychology at the University of North Carolina at Chapel Hill where he teaches both intervention and consultation courses. His research interests include school-based problem-solving teams, professional development, and communicative processes in consultation.

Leslie M. Babinski is an Associate Professor and Director of the School Counseling Program at Bucknell University. Her research interests include teacher professional development and children with learning and behavior problems. She is the co-author of the book *From Isolation to Conversation: Supporting New Teachers' Development.*

Dwight L. Rogers is an Associate Professor in the Elementary Education faculty at the University of North Carolina at Chapel Hill. His research interests include the lived experiences of beginning teachers, caring in the classroom and teacher–child relationships, and classroom discourse. He is the co-author of the book *From Isolation to Conversation: Supporting New Teachers' Development.*

Mary M. Barnett is a school psychologist at Alogonquin Regional High School in Northboro, Massachusetts. She received her master's degree from the University of North Carolina at Chapel Hill and her bachelor's degree in special education from Clemson University.

JOURNAL OF EDUCATIONAL AND PSYCHOLOGICAL CONSULTATION, 14(3&4), 303–328

The Process of Fostering Consultee Development During Instructional Consultation

Steven E. Knotek

University of North Carolina at Chapel Hill

Sylvia A. Rosenfield

University of Maryland at College Park

Todd A. Gravois

University of Maryland at College Park

Leslie M. Babinski

Bucknell University

This investigation examines how the process of instructional consultation (IC) supports consultees' problem-solving and fosters change in how the consultees understand pertinent work problems. The setting was a mid-Atlantic elementary school's Instructional Consultation Team, and the participants were 13 case manager consultants and 5 teacher consultees. A micro-ethnographic research approach was used and 4 primary sources of data collected: interviews, direct observations, consultation documents, and IC training documents. Analysis of the data uncovered 4 general themes related to the participants' problem-solving and evolving understanding of the work issues. In the discussion, the question of how IC is a constructive process that promotes consultees' development is considered.

Correspondence should be addressed to Steve E. Knotek, University of North Carolina at Chapel Hill, School of Education, CB# 3500, Peabody Hall, Chapel Hill, NC 27599-3500. E-mail: sknotek@email.unc.edu

Consultee-centered consultation is unique among the many forms of consultation because of its special emphasis on facilitating change in consultees' understanding of the dilemma brought to consultation. An explicit goal of this form of consultation is for the consultant and consultee to jointly reconceptualize the work problem so as to facilitate the consultee's restoration and improvement of his or her work interaction with the client (Caplan & Caplan, 1993; Knotek & Sandoval, this issue). Changes in consultees' conceptions of the work problem are thought to occur because consultation is, at its core, a constructive act in which the social process is used to facilitate the individuals' active reconceptualization of the consultation dilemma (Sandoval, 1996). Vygotsky's social constructivist theory of the social transmission of intellectual and cultural knowledge is a useful perspective with which to describe the process of consultee change in consultation (Vygotsky, 1978; Wertsch, 1991).

THEORETICAL ORIENTATION

Vygotsky's (1962, 1978) core premise is that higher psychological processes are developed in individuals through their socially mediated acquisition of specialized forms of thinking, such as cogent problem-solving. Three central ideas define the theory. The first of these is that higher mental functions, such as those used in teaching, are social in origin. That is, higher-order learning is fundamentally a social process in which intrapersonal psychological development occurs as a result of exposure to cultural tools (i.e., problem-solving skills) on the interpersonal, social plane (i.e., in the process of consultation). Second, development is mediated through language when an individual is exposed to new ideas or intellectual means through the use and internalization of specialized forms of speech (i.e., psychological terminology). Finally, supportive facilitators or consultants can help people reach higher levels of functioning. This perspective is useful in the study of consultee-centered consultation because of its emphasis on factors that are key to the consultation process: the judicious use of language, thoughtful facilitation, and consultees' internalization of new ways of thinking about complex problems. This constructive process can be used to conceptualize the process of consultees' development in forms of consultation that are consultee-centered.

INSTRUCTIONAL CONSULTATION

Instructional Consultation (IC; Rosenfield, 1987) was originally conceived of as an ecologically grounded model of consultation that incorporated the consultee-centered approach described in Caplan's (1970) model of mental health consultation. It represents a structured and systematic problem-solving process of consultation focused upon the instructional ecology of schools. One of the central goals of IC is to change how consultees (teachers) frame students' school problems away from viewing them as internal, student-centered deficits, toward understanding student learning as a result of the interaction of instruction, task, and student entry skills. The process and aim of consultation within IC is consultee-centered in that the consultation process is designed to foster nonhierarchical facilitation of problem-solving with the aim of expanding the consultees' (teachers') repertoire of means to support their clients (students). IC seeks to foster the consultee's internalization of new conceptions of the problem and to consequently enhance their problem-solving so that it can be generalized to other students.

IC has evolved both as an individual model of consultation service delivery and as a structured model of team service delivery, entitled Instructional Consultation Teams (IC-Teams; Rosenfield & Gravois, 1996). In IC-Teams, each team member is trained and expected to function as an instructional consultant, providing support to individual teachers who request assistance. Evaluation of the efficacy of IC-Teams reveals that they usually result in decreases in the numbers of students placed in special education, that 85% of IC-Team cases meet their goals, and that many classroom teachers who utilize the IC process express high satisfaction with the support they receive (Rosenfield & Gravois, in press). Thus, to some extent we know about the outcomes and effectiveness of the instructional consultation within the IC-Teaming process. However, important questions remain about how the actual process of IC-Teaming works to support these gains.

IC AS SOCIAL CONSTRUCTION
OF KNOWLEDGE

Vygotsky's tenets of the social construction of knowledge are aligned with the goal and process of consultee-centered consultation. Likewise, these tenets can be restated in terms of the process of IC and the development of team members' own understanding as instructional consultants. Development within the social context of the consultation relationship occurs as the interpersonal process supports the redefinition of the consultation dilemma and the consultee acquires a new conception of the consultation problem. Key to consultees' reconceptualization of the consultation dilemma is their acquisition of a new understanding of the problem space (Wertsch, 1990, 1991). From this perspective, the goal of consultation is to flexibly use rational discourse to promote consultees' acquisition of a broader repertoire of problem-solving skills and to facilitate their internalization of a new sense of the problem. Specifically, "what is wrong" is reconceptualized away from internal or external issues related to the students' failings and into a situated problem of instructional mismatch.

PURPOSE OF THE STUDY

In this article we present a subset of the results from an ongoing, longitudinal study examining multiple aspects (i.e., the IC-Team, the consultation relationships) of the IC-Teaming process within an elementary school. Specifically, we examine characteristics of the consultation process between case manager consultants and teacher consultees about their student clients over the course of the 2000 to 2001 academic school year.

This particular site was selected because of ICs central role in the school's academic problem-solving process. In the previous year, when the school was first opened, IC was chosen to be a systemic school-wide means to engage in an integrated and consistent problem-solving process. The school's commitment to the procedure was evident in that five personnel who represented various professional roles were sent for training to be IC facilitators. The number of facilitators trained were exceptional and demonstrated that the school's commitment to IC went across role and title.

In addition, the IC process appeared to be working: (a) the team was classified as "high implementation," which means that the team reached a level of 80% implementation on the IC Level of Implementation scale (Rosenfield & Gravois, 1996); and (b) the majority of students who were served through the IC process were reported to be making instructional progress in their regular education classes (Maple Tree Elementary, 2001).

Student clients appeared to be benefiting from an effective IC process at the fictitiously named Maple Tree Elementary School. However, what about the consultees? Did they also benefit from the consultation? And, if they did benefit, how did participating in IC consultation support their growth? How did the IC process itself support the development of the consultee? In what ways is the IC process consultee-centered? To answer these questions, a micro-ethnographic investigative approach was used and multiple sources of data were collected.

METHOD

Setting

Maple Tree Elementary School is located in a mid-sized town that serves as the county seat in what may be characterized as a rural mid-Atlantic state community. The school is within commuting distance of a large metropolitan area and the county is rapidly becoming suburbanized. Academically, Maple Tree's school district was ranked as a top performer according to an annual State Department of Education Performance Report. Students' performance assessment composite scores for both the school and district were ranked above the state averages.

Demographic information.   The demographic information was obtained from official school district documents and web pages. The ethnic make-up of the school was predominantly White (94%), and African American students made up the largest proportion of minority children (3%), followed by Hispanic students (1.5%). Asian American and Native American students combined together made up 1% of the school population. The total enrollment of the school was 535 students in Grades K to 5.

Although there was limited ethnic diversity in relation to the rest of the district there was socioeconomic diversity with a substantial number of students (15%) coming from families of low socioeconomic status. Students received special services in the following categories: Title I (14.9%), Free or Reduced Meals (13.2%), and Special Education (12.0%). There were no students classified as Limited English Proficient.

History of the IC process at the site.   The formation of the IC-Team actually began the summer before Maple Tree Elementary's first year when five personnel went to the IC Summer Institute for training as IC facilitators.

Although the introduction of the IC process to the school was not entirely smooth, nor reportedly embraced by all of the teachers, it was considered to be effective in providing a school-wide problem-solving process and in reducing the number of inappropriate student referrals for special education evaluation (Gravois, 2000). For example, during the year of the study, 36 students (6.7% of the school's population) were referred to the IC process, and of those only 8 (1.5% of school's population, 22% of those who were referred for IC) were then referred on to the special education team. All of the students referred for special education evaluation met the criteria to receive services under the Individuals with Disabilities Education Act.

Participants   The participants in the study included all of the 13 members of the IC-Team, each of whom functioned as a case manager, as well as five teachers who were consultees. All of the participants were White and female, and their experience levels varied from (a) 31 years of service to 3 years for the case managers, and (b) 13 years of service to first-year teachers for the consultees. Both of these roles had unique features within the IC process at Maple Tree Elementary.

Case manager consultants.   All 13 case managers were members of the IC-Team that met 25 times over 9 months and functioned at the site level to (a) handle administrative issues, (b) facilitate system-level problem-solving and training, and (c) act as a resource to the specific consultation pairs. Of the 13 case managers, 5 were additionally trained at the summer institute as facilitators who would chair the IC-Team. Professional roles represented on the team were diverse and included: administrator (2), resource teacher, instructional language arts teacher, classroom teacher (3), music teacher, special education teacher, speech pathologist, and school psychologist (2). The additional second school psychologist was not assigned to the school. She had volunteered to serve on the team because of a desire to explore the possibilities of initiating IC-Teams at her assigned schools.

Teacher consultees.   The actual consultation, which is the focus of this study, took place between paired dyads of case managers and teachers. Teachers, including the five who volunteered to be interviewed for this study, entered the consultation process by filing out a Request for Assistance Form. Although the IC process was voluntary, teachers were encouraged, where appropriate, to use IC before they referred students to the Student Study Special Education Team.

Once a consultation relationship was entered into, the pair would meet weekly until the concern was resolved or the teacher withdrew from the process. The time and place were negotiated by the two participants. Meetings normally took place at lunch, after school, during preparation periods, or on Thursdays when the school hired a half-day substitute to cover the teachers' classes during their respective consultations. Consultation was considered to be distinct from the teaming process that occurred at the site-level IC-Team. However, the IC-Team could offer guidance to the case manager, and if requested the IC-Team could even meet with the case manager and consultee to provide additional assistance.

Procedure

This is a qualitative study that used a micro-ethnographic approach to investigate how IC supported the development of the consultee (Erickson & Shultz, 1981; Gee & Green, 1998; Trueba & Wright, 1981). This approach was chosen because it focuses on the social and cognitive interactions between small numbers of individuals in specific contexts. Micro-ethnographies are especially well suited to investigating the process of groups (and dyads), and how individuals within them mutually adopt and utilize specialized knowledge, language, and behaviors (Drickson & Shultz, 1981; Patton, 1990).

The unit of study (focal event) was defined as a collaborative problem-solving event, specifically consultation between a case manager and a teacher, in which one member of the school staff consulted with another member. The consultee and consultant discussed how to conceptualize and improve student's functioning in regular education settings.

The first author and primary researcher was a White male university professor, who was also affiliated with the Instructional Consultation Laboratory at the University of Maryland at College Park. Data were collected using a field-based approach of participant-observation to gather the data (Bogdan & Bicklen, 1992). Over the course of the study, the researcher engaged in direct, personal contact with the team members by attending IC meetings, observing classes, and conducting interviews on site. The observer maintained a low profile during actual IC events by not asking questions or otherwise engaging the participants. Objectivity was maintained through the use of peer debriefings and the collection of team member's logs and their official IC documentation.

Forms of data.   Data collection was designed to allow description and analysis of the basic process of consultation within the unique context of the IC-Team. To accomplish this specific task, the following primary sources of data were collected: (a) 20 hr of audio-taped interviews of 17 participants (13 case manager consultants and 5 teacher consultees, including one person who was both a case manager and a teacher consultee, were individually interviewed in sessions ranging in length from 45 to 95 min; see Table 1 for survey format); (b) over 40 hr of direct observations of IC-Team meetings, classroom applications of interventions, and IC consultation data collected with audiotapes at the interviews and field notes in all settings; (c) consultation documents that included the consultant's and the consultee's consultation notes summaries, artifacts (see Table 2 for descriptions), and classroom materials, such as student's work; and (d) IC-Team meeting minutes and materials, yearly reports, and IC training materials (see Table 2 for a description). Additionally, 11 IC-Team meetings were also videotaped. Portions of the meetings in which teacher–case manager dyads discussed a case or their consultation process were recorded and used as a means to cross-check the other data sources in order to further the credibility and reliability of the study.

Validity and reliability.   Credibility was achieved through triangulation with multiple forms of data, and through member-checking and de-

TABLE 1
Examples of the Semi-Structured Interview Questions

Teacher/Consultee interview
    1. These questions are about your experience with the IC process:
        What first motivated you to refer a case to the IC process?
        Please describe the nature of your working relationship with your consultant.
    2. These next questions are about your general opinions about students and their school performance:
        What qualities would you say describe a good student?
        What qualities would you say describe a poor student?
Case manager/Consultant interview
    1. These questions are about your understandings of the purpose and process of IC:
        What are the goal(s) of Instructional Consultation?
        How are these goals(s) accomplished?
    2. These questions are about your use of particular skill sets as an IC Case Manager:
        Before you became a case manager you underwent professional development in which you learned how particular skill sets are applied to the process of IC. Have you found any of these skill sets to be particularly useful in your work as a Case Manager? (If yes, then please elaborate.)
        Have you used any of these skills in other, non-IC, situations? (If yes, then please elaborate.)
    3. These next questions are about your overall experience with IC:
        Please describe your overall experience as a Case Manager.
        What would you say are the core values of IC? (What seems to matter most in this process?)
        What else would you like to share about the IC process?

TABLE 2
Maple Tree Elementary School's Instructional Consultation Documents

Name	Description
Case Documentation Form (CDF)	Dates of contacts, summary of consultation, and date/plans for next meeting.
Student Documentation Form (SDF)	Identifying information and three forms of data: clear behavioral description of the problem, goals and objectives, and intervention(s).
Goal Attainment Scale	Charts progress of case through the 6 core steps.
Operational Definitions	Statement of problem in observable terms, statement of objectives for solving problem, and chart of progress of interventions.
Summary of Meetings	Date, summary, and follow-up.
Satisfaction with Instructional Consultation (SIC)	Evaluation form given to all teachers consisting of two parts: 11 questions on a 5 or 3 point scale asking about teachers' satisfaction with Case Managers, and 9 questions about satisfaction with IC model.
Maple Tree Year End IC Survey (YES)	Staff development document consisting of ratings of understanding IC goals and process and open ended questions.
Needs Assessment: Case Manager (NACM)	Survey given to all Case Managers to assess training needs, 10 areas assessed on 4-point scale.
Summary of IC Cases (SC)	Name, demographic information, referral concerns, outcomes.

briefings with participants (Patton, 2002). As the data were incorporated into the QSR-N6 (Queens, Austrailia; QSR International) data management system, comparisons were made by cross-checking the individual findings from one data source against the thematic units and content that were found in the other data sources (Patton, 2002). Member-checking occurred throughout the investigation as data were collected and reviewed. As the data were collected and initially coded the findings were discussed with team members for their validity and accuracy. Transferability was increased through the use of multiple subjects. Objectivity was increased by the collection of daily process notes and the IC logs (see Table 2 for a description.) Reliability was increased by member-checking across time for content and conclusions.

Data Analysis

The data analysis was aimed at both describing and understanding the consultation process within the unique context of IC. Toward this aim, close attention was paid to descriptions of the process from the perspectives of both the consultant and the consultee, with an eye towards understanding how IC supported the development of the consultees.

Analysis began as the data were initially collected and examined for evidence of recurring topics and process within and across individuals and IC roles (case manager, teacher). Hymes's (1972) SPEAKING paradigm (named from the first letter in each of the axes described next) was used for this initial coding and categorization of the data (see Table 3). This paradigm is useful because it allows a researcher to consider both the context of unique social relationships and their affiliated speech events simultaneously (Cameron, 2001). Transcripts of the interviews, field notes, and documents were coded by their SPEAKING characteris-

TABLE 3
Categorization of IC Speech Events Using Hymes' SPEAKING Grid

Component	Description	Example
Setting and scene		
Setting	Time and place	Conference room, Thursdays 2:30-3:30
Scene	Psychological and cultural setting	Problem-solving group
		Professional development
Participants	Relationships and roles	IC Facilitator, IC case manager, and teacher
Ends and purposes	Goals and outcomes	Develop diverse problem-solving skills
Act sequence	Message form and content	Temperature taking: information, complaints, recommendations, worries/concerns, and appreciations
Key instrumentalities	Overall tone	Reflective, serious, joking
	Spoken and written language	Members' speech, IC worksheets
Norms		
Interactions	How speech proceeds	Case managers' use of questioning
Interpretation	Common knowledge and shared understandings	Mutual understanding of influences on student learning and focus on task-environment match
Genres	Type of speech	Formal Functional, "problem statement"
		Informal greetings, "How are you today?"

tics, and then matched and integrated. Initial categories were developed from this sorting of the data and were primarily coded by the first author.

The integrated data were then electronically imported into the QSRN6 qualitative data management software program along hierarchically indexed nodes of IC role, professional role, and individual. The nodes were selected because they were key components of the unit of study, and they allowed a description and analysis of the consultation process. Next, these categories were coded according to process (i.e., collaborative, directive; Dougherty, 2000; Safran, 1991) and content (i.e., problem descriptors; Rosenfield & Gravois, 1996); the data were then searched for themes and patterns and re-collated along four themed nodes. These data were used to answer the study's questions about how IC supported the consultees' professional development, and in what ways the IC process could be construed as consultee centered.

The final analysis of the data produced four general and recurring themes within the categories: (a) the experience of IC problem-solving as initially paradoxical, (b) the collaborative nature of IC communication and problem solving, (c) conceptual changes regarding consultees' understanding of the problem space and appropriate interventions, and (d) issues related to the process of the consultants relinquishing the expert role in IC. These results are presented in the following section.

RESULTS

A Paradoxical Experience

The philosophical intent of the IC problem-solving process is to help teachers focus on specific, salient, instructionally focused problems over which they have some control, while helping them avoid futile attempts to solve issues over which they have no control (i.e., socioeconomic status of the student; Rosenfield, 1987). The consultation process consists of five stages: entry, problem identification and analysis, intervention planning, intervention implementation, and resolution or termination (Rosenfield & Gravois, 1996).

The IC problem-solving process, especially the problem-identification component, was at first experienced by four of the teachers as paradoxical and counter-intuitive, yet ultimately effective. At the initiation of problem-identification, these teachers resisted what they understood to be attempts to lead them to oversimplify the problem space (Wertsch, 1990).

Teachers were concerned they were being guided to modify their understanding of the student's "multifaceted," "intertwined," and "global" issues, and to instead conceptualize of the salient issue(s) as narrow, data based, and instructionally focused problems.

Two of the teachers initially interpreted the process of narrowing the problem down, and away from student characteristics, as a move away from their view of the student as a "whole child." The following quotation illustrates how one teacher experienced the process of narrowing her focus:

> Definitely, you are focusing on the instruction. It is a support for the teacher and you are looking at those instruction and task, specifically. You really have to focus in, narrow it down to specifics. In that respect, I think that is where you are able to pinpoint. I think as teachers sometimes, we get very global with things because of our frustration, we start encompassing, pulling in everything, and we sometimes tend to neglect what they [students] can do, and [instead] look at what they [students] can't do. Once we get some of those "can dos" in place, and focus on specific areas, that they [students] need to be successful, you can move to that next stage. You are really looking at narrowing it down. (Tina, interview)

Teachers additionally reported that, after their initial reluctance to narrow their focus, when they worked through the process they actually arrived at a workable framework from which to reframe the problem, leave the "real murky water" of the "multifaceted problem definition," and identify a place to begin to work with their students. On the year-end Satisfaction with IC Form (SIC; Table 4), all five teachers reported that they were satisfied with their case manager's support of their problem-identification. Four out of the five teachers also reported that they were satisfied with their case manager's support of their development of useful strategies.

A core and essential aspect of the problem-solving process was recognized as the introduction of the questions to the problem-identification. The consultant would facilitate problem-identification by asking the consultee to consider aspects of the work problem, such as: What can this child do? How does he think? What does he do when he doesn't know what to do? What is it exactly that you are trying to do? What are your goals for the child? What are you really trying to accomplish? (IC Training Manual, 1999). A veteran school psychologist said, "It [The IC process] really forces you to ask questions and then based on the answers you get, to pick a direction to go

TABLE 4
Summary of Results From Teachers' Satisfaction With Instructional
Consultation Form Part I

	Teachers (n = 5)		
Experience With Case Manager	Not Satisfied (n)	Neutral (n)	Satisfied (n)
Access to case manager	0	0	5
Timeliness to requests for assistance	0	1	4
Comfort level with consultant	0	0	5
Understands children's behavior	0	0	5
Supports problem identification	0	0	5
Supports developing strategies	0	1	4
Supports implementing strategies	0	2	3
Overall effectiveness of IC	0	1	4
Total	0	5	35

Notes.   Not Satisfied = Very dissatisfied + Dissatisfied; Satisfied = Satisfied + Very satisfied.

there, and to set a goal. And that's very different than, 'there's overwhelming compelling evidence to test.'" (Kelly, interview). The psychologist's comments describe how the process brought the focus to problem-solving in the service of sharpening the focus of the larger vision.

Two of the teachers reported that they initially resisted the consultants' use of these questions to reconsider their closely held global beliefs about "problem students." To these teachers it seemed paradoxical that such specific questions about a student in such a specific context could lead them to think about the student in a broader, more complex fashion. Ultimately, all of the teachers found that the consultation process allowed them to think through the work problem in such a way as to develop a "meaningful" problem statement, and establish a newly created frame from which to reimagine the situation. The five teachers reported that after participating in the IC process they had acquired confidence to deal with similar problems in the future.

Collaborative Communication

At Maple Tree Elementary School, the IC process is generally viewed as reciprocal in nature, and the participants considered it to be a joint and deeply collaborative process on at least three levels: (a) the mutual communication between case manager and consultee, (b) the joint engagement in the problem-solving process, and (c) the dual responsibility for action.

Overall, the participants perceived their communications as having the qualities of active listening (Rosenfield, 1987), mutual engagement, and turn taking. In their written comments and interview responses, many of the participants cited the fit between the communicative intentions and goals of the case managers and the corresponding experience of the teachers. On both the SIC (Part II, open questions) and the Year End Survey, the majority of the teacher respondents indicated that the collaborative component of the IC process was a "plus" and was "most appreciated." Each of 13 case managers who were interviewed believed it was their responsibility to listen and actually hear what the teacher was saying, and then through the processes of reflecting and clarifying, to talk through the problem with the teacher. To accomplish this goal, communication skills were practiced throughout the school year (Maple Tree Elementary, 9/14, 11/2, and 3/9). Several of the teacher's remarked upon the uniqueness of their IC conversations in the work setting. A new teacher reported:

> Everything that I have to say is always taken very seriously. Even when I have a hard time expressing myself, she will say "What is it exactly that you are trying to do? What are you trying to accomplish? How do you think you can do this?"… She really takes the time to listen and it is not just sitting idly by and being quiet. (Beth, interview)

The participants' perceptions of the communications suggest that they were comfortable enough with the consultation relationship to be honest and forthcoming with one another. Teacher's doubts and concerns were heard and discussed.

In the IC training process (Rosenfield & Gravois, 1996) the case managers learn that both the consultant and the consultee each have a responsibility to engage in the problem-solving. This IC goal of shared responsibility was discussed during three interviews when the participants described an interactive aspect of their problem-solving experience: "throw[ing] things back and forth," "sharing notes," and "brainstorming." The case manager and teacher each have distinct communicative roles. In the IC model, case managers are trained to pose questions, so as to help teachers talk through their presenting problems. Webster, Knotek, Babinski, and Rogers (this issue) describe how important this questioning process is to the consultation. However, as one case manager reported, the communicative roles are not necessarily exclusive: "She [teacher] has been very, very collaborative, very receptive. I have learned as much from her as she has from me" (Shelia, interview). In the IC model, problems are solved through an iterative process that aims to engage team members.

Consultee Change

Case managers understood that the aim of IC was to support classroom teachers to change how they understood and worked with students who were having problems. Shana, a case manager, described the aim of IC: "To help teachers help students" (Interview). As is the case with many forms of consultation, in IC students are thought to be supported indirectly through affirmative changes in the teachers' functioning brought about through the consultation relationship (IC Training Manual, 1999). Case managers emphasized that although the content might vary, their goal was to facilitate a change in the teachers' basic understanding of the work problem, away from student deficiency and towards the efficacy of the current instructional match. During the interviews, 9 of the 13 case managers referenced the IC philosophy of instructional match (IC Training Manual, 1999). This underlying IC conception was first introduced during their training to encourage a shift of attention away from student deficiency and toward issues of the match between student and task, and classroom environment. At Maple Tree Elementary School, comments on the Year End Survey and the SIC (see Table 2 for descriptions of the forms) indicated that participation in IC was affiliated with distinctive and reoccurring types of consultee change, including (a) a shift in focus of concern from global issues to achievable, positive goals; (b) a new understanding of the population of students that could be successful in their regular education classes; and (c) the efficacy of the use of data in planning instruction for students experiencing academic problems.

Shift in focus.   The consultants' use of what the consultees referred to as "the questions" during problem-identification was associated with changes in the teachers' subsequent approach to thinking through work-related problems. This questioning, or problem-framing, was related to teachers' reorientation of the problem away from students' personal and familial deficiencies and toward instructional match. As one teacher remarked:

> I have been through this with a couple of kids now. [The process] is a helpful one, [because] it helps to go back and think about what they can do because naturally you are working with children who are struggling, and sometimes

it is easy to forget that they are making some progress and that there are things that they can do....When you start talking about all of the different things that kids are not doing well,...you [sometimes need to know] what things we can let go for now and not try to work on too much at one time, to really narrow that focus. (Ella, interview)

The shift in the focus was even accompanied by a change in the clarity of the problem. Narrowing in on discrete aspects of the situation allowed the consultee to more thoughtfully plan for change:

I think just being able to look at the data and use it has really helped me. Really helped me a lot, just the visual of seeing, okay, you are doing what you are supposed to do. Whereas, if there is not [any change in the data], then you know that there is something else that you need to do to change that [problem] to make it better. (Tammy, interview)

Who can be supported.   The flexibility in thinking and action that was acquired through the IC process also led some teachers to reassess what kinds of students could be successful in regular education classes. Both case managers and teachers reported a shift in their attitude towards and thinking about problem students. One case manager, Denise, stated that there has been a shift in her attitude about "what kinds of students" can be successful in regular education, noting that "[we] can't just say, 'I am only going to take this top group and you guys deal with the rest [in special education].'" A teacher expressed a complementary sentiment, "It keeps you from just saying 'He is not going to learn anyway, no matter what I do.' It keeps you from doing that and forces you to keep going to bat for that kid and helping him not give up too" (Beth, interview).

Data collection.   The five basic steps of the IC problem-solving process are based upon and revolve around the active collection of baseline data (Rosenfield & Gravois, 1996). A Student Documentation Form (SDF) is used to guide and record the problem-solving process, and the students' actual progress is graphed on a performance chart (Rosenfield & Gravois, 1996). It is through this data-driven process that the teachers' ideas about instructional match and students' functioning are first measured before interventions are acted upon. Every one of the 36 cases referred by teachers to the IC process had a SDF. Many teachers reported being initially uneasy and even resistant to this data-driven approach to solving a work-related problem. Comments about the use of the SDF ranged from "I didn't see the point" to "It [data collection] is very time consuming" (Tammy, interview).

Teachers' skeptical attitudes towards incorporating data in the problem-solving process changed after they went through the process, especially as a result of their case managers' participation in the data collection, as outlined in remarks on the Consultation Documentation Forms (CDFs) and in interviews. The following vignette illustrates this point:

> Ms. Henry, a first-year, second-grade teacher, had invited the primary researcher into her classroom to observe her implement an intervention with a student she had referred into the IC process. The second grader, Marcus, had difficulties with both reading comprehension and emotional outbursts. In this instance, Marcus was observed working on using visual clues to retell a story to increase his comprehension. When the class took a break and went out to recess Ms. Henry picked up a folder of Marcus' SDF forms and sat down. Ms. Henry placed the charts on the table, and pointed to the graphic examples of Marcus progress. "See these lines? These trends? I have parent conferences coming up in a week and I can't wait to show Marcus' mother his progress. This approach is really great, the parent will be able to understand what I've been doing, and hopefully this will help the mother trust me. At first this data thing was really a pain, but Georgina (her case manager) helped me make sense of how I can use all this information." (Field notes)

As both participants jointly took part in the charting, and even the collection of the data, teachers experienced a high degree of affinity for their case managers and the data-gathering process. From the perspective of a second-grade teacher:

> I really didn't [initially] like the data question much....[Although] collecting that data is really helpful now....[Data collection] is the most useful piece to me as an educator....It drives your instruction. [Data] tells you exactly where you need to go and what the child needs to know. It forces you to do that. It really makes you look at what you are doing and to find ways to go. (Tina, interview)

Relinquishing the Expert Role

IC is unique because of the wide range of in-house professionals that assume the role of case manager consultant (Rosenfield & Gravois, 1996). At Maple Tree Elementary the consultants had a variety of professional titles: regular education teacher, music teacher, instructional language arts specialist, speech pathologist, resource teacher, school psychologist, assistant principal, and principal. In addition to their roles as case managers on the IC-Team, the team members all had other, more primary, responsibilities inside the organization. Seven of the case managers' professional roles were that of specialists (e.g., school psychologists and resource teachers) in which they provided expert opinion and service to students and regular education teachers. Fulfilling the duties of consultant proved to be a challenge to many of these specialists because the role definition and duties of a case manager ran counter to the expert duties associated with their usual professional practice.

In IC, the consultant's primary task is facilitation of consultee change through the process of collaborative consultation. The collaborative give-and-take of this iterative, nonhierarchical process diverged from the normal professional practice of the specialists. Instead of being in an authoritarian stance in relation to the teachers, the case managers had to reconfigure their professional relationship to be more collaborative and egalitarian (IC Training Manual, 1999). The focus of their responsibility in the professional situation shifted from telling teachers about their students to concentrating on the teachers' beliefs and perspectives and asking teachers to be the authority regarding the student (CDFs). Some of the specialists found this shift from expert to consultant to be demanding:

> Even though I know the whole IC process is to first be an IC consultant and [engage in] listening, I had to force myself to [listen] more, because as a reading specialist sometimes teachers come up and say "I have this problem," and then you [the specialist] want to come up with the solution....So at first I wanted to jump right in and say, "This is what you should do, and this is what you should do." Boy, stepping back, that was very hard. (Denise, interview)

After the specialists began consulting and experienced collaboration, they became more comfortable and trusted the process:

> I really like this [collaboration] and I really appreciate the whole IC process because sometimes you are stumped and sometimes you [as the specialist] don't know what the solution is. Sometimes when you really look at the problem, and what the teacher thinks is the problem, and work through all the [problem-solving] steps, [then you] find out the problem isn't really what you thought it was, that's what's good about IC. This process really takes the pressure off a special education person, speech person, reading specialist. (Shana, interview)

There was a consensus among the specialists that because collaboration was iterative and content free, that it fostered flexibility in thinking and opened up unseen possibilities with which to better serve the students.

The experience reported by the two school psychologists exemplifies how the specialists describe this shift.

School psychologists.   Some of the specialists, especially the school psychologists, found their experience with IC had a major impact on what they believed were the strictures of their professional practice. The bread-and-butter of many school psychologists' professional practice is special education assessment (Reschly & Ysseldyke, 1995) in which the medical model is used to frame the functioning of students. The focus of the psychologist is on detecting any deficits in the students' functioning and helping to determine if a special education placement is in order. The Maple Tree psychologists both reported that when they were in the role of case manager, they began to reconceptualize their default professional responsibility away from special education assessment and toward academic problem-solving. Even though they were not instructional experts, as they took part in the collaborative process, the school psychologists also believed they were stakeholders in the instructional process. Trudy, a school psychologist remarked:

> I have learned more in the past 2 years [about reading instruction] than I have learned in the past 20 years, I have to tell you, about education, about teaching, about reading. I just never considered that anything I really had to know about....I am not there yet [in fully understanding the instructional practice] … but I am feeling we can talk the same language. … It has affected my role as a school psychologist in the rest of my job because it has changed my thinking about taking the focus off what is wrong with the student. (Trudy, interview)

Expectations about professional role, content, and process began to shift as the case manager specialists collaborated with their consultee teachers. Case managers came to value their additional role as collaborative facilitator, began to rethink and reevaluate the etiology of student's academic troubles, and deepened their appreciation of collaboration's potential to support teacher's ability to solve their work-related problems.

DISCUSSION

In addition to investigating how IC supported consultee's development, one of the challenges in the current study of consultation was to learn more about the process of particular forms of consultation, especially to ascertain how the consultative process hypothesized in a model's theory actually unfolds in practice (Brown, Pryzwansky & Schulte, 2001). There needs to be more investigation regarding the congruency between theory and practice.

The results of the study discussed here show that IC at Maple Tree Elementary is a collaborative process that supports problem-solving and fosters change in how both the teachers and the case managers understand and carry out their professional duties. Based upon these results, IC meets the constructivist criteria of fostering consultee development within a collaborative relationship (Knotek & Sandoval, this issue). However, what qualities inherent in IC consultation are actually constructive?

It may be argued that what makes IC a constructive undertaking are three of the traits theoretically central to forms of consultee-centered consultation (Caplan & Caplan, 1993; Caplan, Caplan, & Erchul, 1995; Sandoval, 1996): (a) effective alliance building, (b) orderly reflection, and (c) the generation of alternative hypotheses. Together these traits may be thought to characterize the process needed to meet the aims of consultee-centered consultation. When an effective alliance (relationship) is established, the consultant can facilitate (orderly reflection) an examination of the issues, through which new conceptions (alternate hypotheses) of the work problem emerge. Were these three traits present in the IC process at Maple Tree Elementary School? How did the practice of IC underpin the consultees' development?

Effective Alliance Building

A basic premise of consultee-centered consultation, and IC as one of its forms, is that consultee change occurs within the context of a nonhierarchical relationship between two professionals. The creation of an effective relationship, or consultation alliance, is a prerequisite for the kind of socially mediated problem-solving that IC is based upon. If a teacher is to freely construct new ideas about a situation in her classroom, she must not feel judged, evaluated, or otherwise constrained by the consultant. Problem-solving must occur within an accepting, supportive environment so that a teacher may spend consultation time constructing new possibilities and not defending old practices.

The development of the consultees' thinking and behavior that occurred during the IC process at Maple Tree Elementary suggests that the basic conditions necessary for a collaborative alliance were in place during consultation. Some of the results from the present study suggest how the IC process supports the formation of an alliance. First, the consultees at Maple

Tree Elementary valued the way they were talked to by their case managers. Through the process of active listening, the teachers had the experience of being heard. Second, teachers believed they were part of a reciprocal process. Both the case managers and teachers understood the IC process to consist of interaction between partners and reported the collaboration was conducted through turn-taking and sharing. Finally, the teachers' believed that their perspectives on the work problem were of paramount importance in the IC process. Consultants consistently asked the consultees for their perspective of the work problem, and these perspectives ultimately decided the kinds of data collected and interventions implemented.

Together, these three traits helped form the alliance upon which the collaborative problem-solving would take place. Given some teachers' initial resistance to some aspects of the process, especially their initial misgivings about the paradoxical reframing of the problem and the data gathering, establishment of an alliance was a necessary precondition to the IC process.

Orderly Reflection, Alternative Hypotheses, and Conceptual Change

A baseline aim of IC, and all forms of consultee-centered consultation, is to support conceptual change on the part of consultees, so as to improve their ability to handle present as well as future work problems. To accomplish this task, the goal is to use the consultative relationship to support the consultees' conceptual change. The four themes in the results section identify traits within IC that facilitate the consultees' social construction of knowledge: (a) the process of reframing the problem from global issues and deficiency to instructional match, (b) the collaborative nature of the communications (social facilitation of a new problem space), (c) collection of data to objectively construct a representation of the students' functioning, and (d) the use of collaborative thinking to create a more thorough understanding of the issues.

Reframing the problem.   Prior to their engagement in IC many of the teachers understood the work problem in terms of global issues and students' deficiencies. However, at the beginning of the IC process, teachers were introduced to the concept of instructional match as an influence on student learning. This construct, that students' learning problems could be accounted for by instructional variables, added another dimension to the consultees' representation of the problem. Focusing on instructional match as a problem required many of the teachers to examine their assumptions about the etiology of students' functioning, and to begin to create new representations of the work problem.

Collaborative communications.   The IC process is designed to be interactive and to foster a joint engagement in the problem-solving process. Ultimately, the case consultant and the consultee talk through the issues and socially co-construct a new interpretation of the problem space. From a Vygotskian perspective, IC's social structure fostered the consultees' engagement in a new form of scientific thinking (Wertsch, 1991).

Collection of data.   Conceptual development is thought to occur through the amassing of evidence that favors one view and that also effectively counters a previously held view (Gopnick & Wellman, 1994; Kuhn, 1989). If a new concept is found to be more utilitarian than a previous one, the previous conception is dropped or modified, and the new concept is then adopted. The collection of data during problem-identification and analysis provided the consultees with such a process. Teachers reported the collection of data allowed them to identify problems and plan instruction. Additionally, they found that the process itself helped them to reevaluate their thinking about the ability of problem students to function in regular education. The collection of objective data during IC allowed the teachers to not only challenge and change some of their subjective beliefs about the etiology of students' problems, but also served to increase their sense of the range of students they could successfully accommodate in their classrooms.

Alternative hypotheses.   Although the generation of alternative hypotheses is often listed as a separate trait in the literature on consultee-centered consultation, in IC it is part and parcel of the process of orderly reflection and is best discussed as an integrated piece of orderly reflection (Caplan & Caplan, 1993; Rosenfield & Gravois, 1996).

Generation of alternative hypotheses occurs in IC as the consultant guides the consultee to collect particular forms of data, as they co-construct knowledge using a problem-solving framework, and as the frame of reference is widened. The IC consultant does not guide the consultee to collect data about the dysfunctional process of a child's home. Rather, she supports the consultee's collection of data about the instructional match between a student and his or her educational environment. The conceptualization of the problem, collection of data, and generation of interventions does not occur in a random fashion. Instead, the consultant actively questions the consultee and models a problem-solving process. Finally, through the focus on instructional match, the consultant suggests an additional frame of reference from which to understand the work problem.

Taken together, IC's traits of reframing the etiology of the problem, the consultants' use of questions to guide the instructional conversation, the collection of data to confirm or disconfirm ideas, the iterative brainstorming, and the generation of alternative hypotheses resulted in a process of orderly reflection that supported the construction of new understandings of and approaches to the workplace problem.

LIMITATIONS

The ethnographic approach used in this investigation is useful in describing and analyzing aspects of the process of consultation. It allowed for a close examination of what occurs during consultation and an exploration of how the process is experienced by the participants. However, as with all single-site studies, questions may arise about the generalizability of the findings. Are these results useful in describing the process of IC in other settings?

Although there are undoubtedly differences between the context of IC at Maple Tree Elementary and the contexts of other schools, the core philosophy, methods, and goals remain the same from site to site. Namely, other schools use consultation as a collaborative means to support teachers in their support of students. In this respect, the general themes found in the data may be generalizable across contexts.

However, it is reasonable to suspect that the relatively strong adoption of the IC process at Maple Tree Elementary is not representative of the situation at other schools. What happens to the consultative relationship if the administration does not support the process, or if the school culture is overly punitive towards its teachers? What happens in a school that has a different proportion of high-versus low-achieving students? What happens at sites that have numerous teachers who are teaching on emergency credentials? Will the IC structure be able to meet the hypothetically greater needs of these teachers? Therefore, future studies should investigate the process in other contexts, such as low-income, inner-city schools.

Methodological limitations include the omission of recordings of the actual consultation process. The data presented in this study were in part based upon the perceptions of the participants. Credibility would have been enhanced with the use of an external auditor.

In addition, because this study focused on describing and understanding how IC supports consultees, it could not adequately address questions about the shortcomings within the process. IC is not a panacea and some concerns did arise, including the amount of time necessary to participate in the IC process and the focus on a small number of students at a time. Finally, the gender and ethnic makeup of the team was very homogeneous, consisting of White, female educators. This sample is not representative of the faculty makeup of many schools. These concerns warrant further exploration and future research

REFERENCES

Bogdan, R., & Biklen, S. (1992). *Qualitative research for education: An introduction to theory and methods.* Needham Heights, MA: Allyn & Bacon.

Brown, D., Pryzwansky, W., & Shulte, A. (2001). *Psychological consultation: Introduction to theory and practice* (5th ed.). Boston, MA: Allyn & Bacon.

Cameron, D. (2001). *Working with spoken discourse.* London: Sage.

Caplan, G. (1970). *The theory and practice of mental health consultation.* New York: Basic Books.

Caplan, G., & Caplan, R. B. (1993). *Mental health consultation and collaboration.* San Francisco: Jossey-Bass.

Caplan, G., Caplan, R., & Erchul, W. P. (1995). A contemporary view of mental consultation: Comments on *Types of Mental Health Consultation. Journal of Educational and Psychological Consultation, 6,* 23–30.

Dougherty, A. M. (2000). *Psychological consultation and collaboration in school and community settings* (3rd ed.). Belmont, CA: Brooks/Cole.

Erickson, F., & Shultz, J. (1981). When is a context? Some issues and methods in the analysis of social competence. In J. Green & C. Wallat (Eds.), *Ethnography and language in educational settings* (pp. 147–160). Norwood, NJ: Ablex.

Gee, J. P., & Green, J. L. (1998). Discourse analysis, learning, and social practice: A methodological study. In P. D. Pearson & A. Iran-Nejad (Eds.), *Review of Research in Education, 23,* 119–169. Washington, DC: AERA.

Gopnick, A., & Wellman, H. M. (1994). The theory theory. In L. A. Hirschfeld & S. A. Gelman (Eds.), *Mapping the mind: Domain specificity in cognition and culture* (pp. 257–293). New York: Cambridge University Press.

Gravois, T. A. (2000). *Goals 2000: Year end report.* College Park, MD: Instructional Consultation Laboratory, University of Maryland.

Gravois, T. A, Knotek, S. E., & Babinski, L. M. (2002). Educating practitioners as consultants: The instructional consultation team consortium. *Journal of Educational and Psychological Consultation, 13,* 113–132.

Gravois, T. A., & Rosenfield, S. A. (1999). *Instructional consultation training manual.* College Park, MD: Instructional Consultation Laboratory.

Gravois, T. A., & Rosenfield, S. A. (2002). A multi-dimensional framework for the evaluation of instructional consultation teams. *Journal of Applied School Psychology, 19*(1), 5–29.

Hymes, D. (1972). Models of interaction of language and social life. In J. Gumperz & D. Hymes (Eds.), *Directions in sociolinquistics: The ethnography of communication* (pp. 35–71). New York: Hold, Rinehart, & Winston.

Kuhn, D. (1989). Children and adults as intuitive scientists. *Psychological Review, 96*, 674–689.

Maple Tree Elementary School. (2001). *Year-end Instructional Consultation summary report.* College Park, MD: Instructional Consultation Team Laboratory.

Patton, M. Q. (1990). *Qualitative evaluation and research methods* (2nd ed.). Newbury Park, CA: Sage.

Patton, M. Q. (2002). *Qualitative research & evaluation methods* (3rd ed.). Thousand Oaks, CA: Sage.

Reschly, D. J., & Ysseldkye, J. E. (1995). School psychology paradigm shift. In A. Thomas & J. Grimes (Eds.), *Best practices in school psychology III* (pp. 17–32). Washington, DC: National Association of School Psychologists.

Rosenfield, S. A. (1987). *Instructional consultation.* Hillsdale, NJ: Lawrence Erlbaum Associates, Inc.

Rosenfield, S. A,. & Gravois, T. A. (1996). *Instructional consultation teams: Collaborating for change.* New York: Guilford.

Safran, S. P. (1991). The communication process and school-based consultation: What does the research say? *Journal of Educational and Psychological Consultation, 8,* 93–100.

Sandoval, J. (1996). Constructivism, consultee-centered consultation and conceptual change. *Journal of Educational and Psychological Consultation, 7,* 89–97.

Trueba, H. T., & Wright, P. G. (1981). On ethnographic studies and multicultural education. *NABE Journal, V*(2), 29–56.

Vygotsky, L. (1962). *Thought and language.* Cambridge, MA: Harvard University Press.

Vygotsky, L. V. (1978). *Mind in society: The development of higher psychological processes.* Cambridge, MA: Harvard University Press.

Wertsch, J. (1990). Negotiating sense in the zone of proximal development. In M. Schwebel, C. Maher, & N. Fagley (Eds.,) *Promoting cognitive development over the life span* (pp. 71–88). Hillsdale, NJ: Lawrence Erlbaum Associates, Inc.

Wertsch, J. (1991). *Voices of the mind: A sociocultural approach to mediated action.* Cambridge, MA: Harvard University Press.

Steven E. Knotek is an Assistant Professor in the School Psychology Program at the University of North Carolina at Chapel Hill where he teaches courses in intervention and consultation. His research interests include professional development of educators, problem-solving teams in schools, and consultee-centered consultation.

Sylvia A. Rosenfield is the Co-Director of the Laboratory for IC-Teams and a Professor in the School Psychology Program at the University of Maryland at College Park. Her research interests include school consultation services, instructional consultation, and urban education. She is the co-author of *Instructional Consultation Teams: Collaborating for Change.*

Todd A. Gravois is Research Associate and Co-Director the Laboratory for IC-Teams at the University of Maryland. His research and practice interests include training, implementation, and evaluation of consultation-based services in schools; problem-solving teams, and curriculum-based assessment. He is co-author *of Instructional Consultation Teams: Collaborating for Change* and the chapter "Best Practices in Curriculum Based Assessment" published in *Best Practices in School Psychology.*

Leslie M. Babinski is an Associate Professor and Director of the School Counseling Program at Bucknell University. Her research interests include teacher professional development and children with learning and behavior problems.

JOURNAL OF EDUCATIONAL AND PSYCHOLOGICAL CONSULTATION, 14(3&4), 329–362

Multicultural Consultee-Centered Consultation: When Novice Consultants Explore Cultural Hypotheses With Experienced Teacher Consultees

Colette L. Ingraham
San Diego State University

Using case study qualitative methodology and naturalistic inquiry, this study investigates how beginning consultants use multicultural consultee-centered consultation (MCCC) to explore cultural hypotheses with experienced teachers. The study involves the conceptualizations and detailed records of 3 ethnically diverse novice consultants who hypothesize cultural issues in the problem situation and use MCCC with teachers of diverse students ages 6-12. Grounded in the multicultural consultation framework (Ingraham, 2000), analyses focus on consultation stages, communication processes, factors associated with success and failure, and their relationship with co-constructing problem definitions with consultees. Results of within-case and cross-case analyses illustrate the complexity of practicing and studying MCCC and suggest several issues that may influence multicultural consultation outcomes. Specific questions for future research are identified.

New conceptualizations emerge as consultation theories and approaches are applied within a multicultural context (Ingraham & Meyers, 2000). Ingraham (2000) illustrated how the use of a multicultural lens opens a wide range of topics and issues for consideration in culturally diverse set-

---

Correspondence should be addressed to Colette Ingraham, San Diego State University, Department of Counseling and School Psychology, 5500 Campanile Drive, San Diego, CA 92182. E-mail: ingraham@mail.sdsu.edu

tings. When one or more members of the consultation system (e.g., consultant, consultees, clients) are culturally different from the others, a host of issues and processes within the arena of cross-cultural consultation (CCC) arise. In today's schools, there is often diversity within members of the consultation system and consultation theories that are inclusive of cultural diversity are needed to understand the complexity of issues that arise in such situations (Tarver Behring & Ingraham, 1998). Rogers et al. (1999) argued that cultural competence for school psychologists includes raising culturally grounded hypotheses and educating others about cultural issues affecting learning and achievement. How can consultants work to educate teachers about cultural issues? What approaches can consultants use to support teacher development of cultural competence? What aspects of the consultation process are central in working with cultural issues? Proponents of a constructivist approach (e.g., Hylander, 2000; Sandoval, in press) suggest that co-construction of the problem definition and case conceptualization are central in CCC. Multicultural consultation is well suited to promoting conceptual change and new understandings through co-construction (Ingraham, 2000; in press).

To date, quantitative analog designs and qualitative case study methods investigate some aspects of multicultural consultation, but CCC remains relatively unexplored. Analog studies focus on racial factors in consultant–consultee interactions within school psychology (Duncan & Pryzwansky, 1993; Naumann, Gutkin, & Sandoval, 1996; Rogers, 1998), but these are not specific to a CCC approach. Much like the emergent transformation from postpositivistic and quantitative to constructionist and qualitative methods and paradigms occurring within counseling psychology (e.g., Ponterotto, 2002; Pope-Davis et al., 2002), consultation researchers are increasingly looking to qualitative methods to study some of the complexities of culture and consultation. Qualitative methods were used effectively to examine CCC (Hylander, 2000), multicultural consultation (Tarver Behring, Cabello, Kushida, & Murguia, 2000), the use of interpreters in instructional consultation (Lopez, 2000), and consultation overseas (Maital, 2000; Nastasi, Vargas, Berstein, & Jayasena, 2000).

There are several reasons that make case studies the method of choice for inquiry in CCC cases. Lincoln and Guba (1985) propose that case studies provide the "thick description" important for judgments of transferability, demonstrate the interplay between the inquirer and respondents, and provide a grounded assessment of context so readers can more fully understand contextual information. Erlandson, Harris, Skipper, and Allen (1993) recommend case studies for "*emic* inquiry (reconstruction of the respondent's constructions), while conventional report seems better suited for a priori *etic* inquiry" (p. 164). Case studies have illustrated issues and constructs of multicultural consultation (Gibbs, 1980; Ingraham, 2000, in press; Ingraham & Tarver Behring, 1998; Soo-Hoo, 1998), but research on cultural issues in CCC is needed.

The literature reveals that the relationship between culture and the consultation process is multifaceted and complex (Henning-Stout, 1994; Ingraham, 2000; Ingraham & Meyers 2000; Pinto, 1981; Ramirez, Lepage, Kratochwill, & Duffy, 1998; Rogers, 2000; Soo-Hoo, 1998; Tarver Behring & Ingraham, 1998), as is the relationship between cultural competence and counseling (e.g., Sue, Ivey, & Pedersen, 1996). Sue's (2001) multidimensional model of cultural competence for psychology posits a 3 × 4 × 5 cube with critical dimensions that include racial- and culture-specific competence, components of cultural competence, and foci or level of cultural competence. Culture is not a one-dimensional variable but rather a context that permeates the consultation relationship and processes (Ingraham & Tarver Behring, 1998). A multitude of factors can contribute to the outcomes of consultation, including characteristics of the consultant, consultee, presenting problem, methods used in consultation, and relationship between consultant and consultee. Some authors have identified consultant competencies needed for multicultural consultation (Brown, 1997; Gibbs, 1980; Harris, 1991; Ingraham, 2000; Ramirez, et al., 1998; Rogers, 2000; Tarver Behring & Ingraham, 1998) or collaboration (Harris, 1996).

The multicultural consultation framework (see Ingraham, 2000, for a thorough discussion) focuses on the structures and processes within multicultural and cross-cultural consultation. The framework guides consultants to consider a host of potential issues that can arise in multicultural consultation and suggests strategies to increase consultation effectiveness. The five components of the framework include: Eight domains of consultant learning and development (e.g., understanding own and other cultures, approaches for cross-cultural consultation), four domains of consultee learning and development (knowledge, skill, perspective, and confidence), cultural variations in the consultation constellation, contextual and power influences, and specific methods for supporting consultee and client success. Ingraham (2002) also teaches consultants to attend to their own and their consultees' styles of communication to increase trust and rapport and to reduce perceived resistance in consultation. Two styles of communication are taught to highlight differences that can emerge: (a) indirect communication, where one prefers a gentle, non-threatening, more reserved, polite form of discourse; and (b) direct communication, where one prefers to get to the point, without much prefacing, background, or inference required for interpretation. Effective consultants need to learn and use both types of communication to develop rapport with consultees who may strongly prefer one mode or another (Ingraham, 2002). Multicultural consultee-centered consultation (MCCC) combines the multicultural consultation framework with a focus on consultee development when the consultee is culturally different from the student, consultant, or both. Consultants assess (based on Ingraham's 2000 adaptation of Caplan & Caplan, 1993) the consultee's and their own needs for increased knowledge, skill, perspective, and confidence following each consultation session. This assessment guides their intervention with the consultee. While MCCC is useful for developing consultant skills (Ingraham, 2002), research with real consultation cases is needed to explore more fully how these multifaceted and complex processes and relationships are revealed in naturalistic settings.

The purpose of this article is to present a qualitative study of MCCC in schools. The study seeks to explore the following research questions:

1. What happens when beginning consultants try to use MCCC to explore cultural hypotheses with experienced teachers?
2. How are factors in the multicultural consultation framework (Ingraham, 2000) associated with success and failure in CCC?
3. When consultants hypothesize cultural issues in the problem situation, what strategies do they use in their CCC, and how do these strategies work in co-constructing problem definitions with their consultees?

METHOD

Through the use of multiple-case study methodology with embedded units of analysis (Scholz & Tietje, 2002; Yin, 1998), MCCC is examined within a series of consultation sessions that composed the consultation cases of three culturally diverse beginning female consultants, their experienced teacher consultees, and their male and female clients (pupils). Following the recommendations of Sue (1999) and Wampold, Licktenberg, and Waehler (2002), information is reported about the consultants, consultees, clients, and the researcher, thereby giving some context regarding their perspectives and backgrounds. Wampold et al. (2002) argue that it is critical to describe the persons delivering the interventions, particularly with diverse client populations, because variance due to the interventionist can account for up to 90% of the outcome.

Each case summary includes descriptions of the consultant, consultee, and student. The researcher and author is a female European American of mixed heritage (French, Irish, German, English, Scotch, Dutch), was raised in northern California, is in her 40s, has specialized in multicultural issues for over 15 years, and teaches in a culturally diverse graduate program in southern California. These cases were selected because of their use of MCCC with a goal for conceptual change, from among a sample of cases that used Ingraham's (2000) multicultural school consultation framework. Although a complete presentation of each case and method of analysis is beyond the scope of this article, three case summaries and a discussion are presented to provide thick descriptions of some of the complexities and contexts within which these consultation cases evolved.

Data Sources

Consultants in their second year of graduate school were learning to provide consultation to teachers through a year-long course and practicum in school placements. They prepared individual case studies according to a five-page semi-structured protocol, based on Ingraham's (2000) framework (see Table 1 for sample questions). The instructor observed, coached, and evaluated consultants through the use of written critiques, audio-tapes, transcribed consultation sessions, in-class deconstructions, role play, and debriefings.

Data for the studies include extensive portfolios written by consultants with case notes; formative and summative written reflections; consultant analyses; consultant ratings of self and consultee; detailed summative case studies; and, when available, client work samples and outcomes such as follow-up interviews with consultees and observations of clients. All consultants responded to the same semi-structured case note format about the consultation strategies they used, their reflections on the process, and perceived consequences. (Readers can write to Ingraham for a copy.) After each consultation session, and at the conclusion of all sessions, consultants also completed a 7-point rating scale about their own level and their assessment of the consultee's level of knowledge, skill, objectivity, and confidence. Consultants corroborated these numerical ratings, ranging from 1 (*strong need for development*) to 7 (*not a need*), with written evidence such as direct quotations, consultant observations, and narratives about each session. Due to space limitations, an analysis of the formative and summative data from the 7-point ratings of perceived needs for development is not reported in this study.

TABLE 1

Sample Questions Consultants Addressed in Their Consultation Case Analyses, Based on Ingraham's (2000) Framework

---

Dimensions of diversity
1. How did various dimensions of diversity emerge in this case? Describe the nature of the diversity, who was involved, and how it may have influenced the consultation process.
2. Describe the preferred style of communication of yourself and the consultee. Were there any differences in your styles and preferences for communication? If yes, describe.
3. What aspects of the consultee's identity (individual, group, universal) and culture were made salient in the consultation and how were these salient?
4. If you or the consultee used any bridging approaches as a means to build connections across dimensions of diversity, what approaches were used? By whom? How did they work?

Contextual and power influences
5. Describe any contextual and power influences involved with this consultation case. Include attention to influences by the larger society and disruptions in the balance of power, if any.

Methods for supporting consultee and client success
6. Describe any methods you used to support the consultee and/or client's success.

Adjustments in the Consultation Model
7. Did you make any adjustments in the consultation approaches described in your textbooks to adjust the consultation to the culture or needs of the consultee and/or client? If so, describe what you did differently and what effect you think it had on the consultation process.

Learning from reflection
8. What did you observe about yourself in this case? How does this experience inform your future consultation practice? What mistakes did you make with this case and how did you learn from these?
9. Other Comments or Reflections.

Note. A complete list of questions is available from the author.

Consultants were instructed that the purpose of the case analysis was to demonstrate a complete conceptualization of a multicultural consultation case, from beginning to end, and to report on the key aspects of the case that influenced its outcomes. Discussion included what occurred during the consultation case, how the various aspects of the case relate to each other, and the final outcome. In the first part, consultants documented and reflected on a wide range of themes in a semi-structured written paper that included a description of the consultation constellations and members, models used, initial hypotheses and basis, means of problem identification and related components, description of the intervention, who developed it, and how it went. In the second part of the case analyses, consultants completed a 4 × 3 matrix with written documentation to support their evaluation of the consultees' and their own needs for knowledge, skill, objectivity, and confidence. For each of these four areas, consultants included quotes from their consultation sessions when possible, and specific written responses including: (a) a description of what led them to hypothesize consultee needs in each area; (b) what approaches they took, if any, to address the need; and (c) how the consultee responded to the approaches. This matrix was followed by a series of inquiries that asked consultants to reflect on their cases and address questions regarding specific components of Ingraham's (2000) framework (see Table1).

Contextual information about each school site, demographics of the school's student and teacher populations, and other indicators of school climate and achievement were documented as well. Consultants and Ingraham used contextualizing strategies to understand these data in context and search "for relationships that connect statements and events within a context into a coherent whole" (Maxwell, 1996, p. 79). Thus, factors related to a particular school environment, consultant, and consultee were considered, in combination with themes emerging from the cases.

Design and Procedures

Following the conclusion of the consultation course, nine consultants consented to contribute their extensive portfolios, which included summative case studies, formative case notes, and reports from each consultation session to the database used in this project. Ingraham screened this pool to identify cases in which the consultant hypothesized cultural issues related to the problem identification and sought conceptual change in the consultee through MCCC. Four cases met these criteria, but one of the consultants elected not to participate in this study.

Each of the three participating consultants was evaluated by the instructor as demonstrating good skills in listening, communicating, asking relevant consultation questions, and having solid knowledge and skills in eco-systemic assessment-for-intervention that attends to cultural context, learning, and behavioral issues. Written and oral evaluations by field supervisors for each of the three consultants' supervisors corroborated the instructor's assessment of their strengths in consultation, counseling, and communication with staff.

To reduce the potential for bias of consultant trainees commenting on their cases or their instructor's interpretation while they were still in the graduate program, the formal member-checking phases of this study were initiated following the graduation and employment of each consultant. Ingraham developed case summaries, based on an integration of the session notes and summaries, case analyses, demographic information of each school site obtained from a California Department of Education website, and debriefings with the consultant. These case summaries were designed to convey the richness of data available about each consultation system and to add to thickness of description and contextual dimensions to assist readers in determining transferability of the research (Erlandson et al., 1993; Lincoln & Guba, 1985; Yin, 1998).

Following Lincoln and Guba's (1985) recommendations for review and revision for first case drafts, these written case summaries were reviewed and verified by the consultant for each case. Consultants were sent a copy of the summary draft for their case and were asked questions such as: Is it accurate? Does it represent what happened? Are the interpretations on track or off base? Are there other thoughts or interpretations you have about it? Ingraham modified the cases per feedback from the consultants. In one instance, a consultant questioned an ethnic term used in the case summary, thinking it might have been a different word to describe the consultee's ethnicity. In this situation, the original case notes and case study written by the consultant were compared with the summary draft and the consultant and researcher used the term consistent with these notes.

In addition, consultants were asked about their desired level of participation in this research study. Consultants had originally consented to contribute their case notes, consultation session transcripts, session notes, and case analysis. At the beginning of the qualitative study, following Erlandson et al. (1993), consent was renegotiated with the specific purpose of this research and the comprehensive member-checking process it would entail. All agreed to participate and contribute through the member-checking processes. Consultants were given the choice to participate anonymously, to be named as consultant, or to participate as a co-author in writing the research. Due to the demands of their employment as full-time school psychologists, all elected to be named as consultants. Thus, each consultant is identified by name, with her permission, in the acknowledgments and in the footnotes of this article. Confidentiality is maintained regarding the identity of individual consultees, student clients, and schools.

A second level of member checks involved the consultants' participation in identifying and reviewing themes across the cases. Following the data analysis procedures outlined by Creswell (1994; e.g., simultaneous data coding and analysis, data reduction and interpretation, developing matrices, and coding information into themes and categories), Ingraham studied the case files to develop tentative themes of consistency and differences across the three cases. The methods of constant comparison (continuous and simultaneous collection and processing of data) and negative case analysis (continuously refining hypotheses until they account for all known cases without exception; Lincoln & Guba, 1985) were used to continually construct categories and explore hypothesized and emerging relationships among the elements of the three cases. Additionally, other cases by the same consultants were examined to explore potential patterns across consultees for the same consultant. Examples of questions that were explored and ruled out as contributing factors were: Was this the first consultee this consultant worked with? Did the consultant explore cultural issues with any or all of their consultees? Were there differences in the ages or levels of experiences of the consultees? After review of the formative and summative data for these three cases and other cases by the same consultants, these questions were dismissed as not relevant to the present pattern of results. Categories and patterns that showed differences in the successful and unsuccessful cases were retained. These categories and patterns were compared via a *matrix method* (Miles & Huberman, 1984), a comparison across cases showing themes and categories used in coding (see Table 2 for some matrix items). These tentative themes were explored and corroborated in subsequent debriefings with each consultant as part of the member-checking processes. Among these initial themes were considerations regarding the use of self-disclosure; consultant characteristics; consultee characteristics; co-construction of problem definition; methods for supporting consultee conceptual change, which were derived from Ingraham's (2000) framework; and initial readings of these three cases. For example, if the case file did not contain information to reveal if the consultant sought feedback from the instructor or peers during the case, the researcher asked the consultant in these post-verification debriefings. Other follow-up questions the researcher asked consultants included: Did you bring this case to seminar for peer consultation or instructor coaching? Did you continue with the case following your written case study for the course? If so, how were you involved and how did it go? What was the outcome of this case? Do you know of any follow-up information about the teacher consultee or student? If so, please describe. Did you use self-disclosure? If so, can you describe how that went? You described your (or the consultee's) ethnicity as European American; can you tell me which cultures of heritage that involves? Following the collection of these data, a draft of the matrix was shared with consultants to seek their feedback and to make any needed corrections.

TABLE 2
Sample Factors of Difference Across Three Multicultural Consultee-Centered Consultation Cases

Characteristic	Case 1	Case 2	Case 3
Consultation constellation	Consultant–client similarity	Consultant–consultee similarity	Consultee–client similarity
Commonalities (potential bridges with consultant-consultee)	Same gender; both bilingual (with different languages)	Same gender and macro-group ethnicity	Both exposed to cultural difference within upbringing
Additional differences among consultants-consultees	Ethnicity	Perspective about culture	Gender, ethnicity
Model(s) used	Mental health, instructional	Mental health, behavioral	Instructional, mental health
Client student ethnicity and gender	Vietnamese born male	U.S.-born African American and Mexican American female	U.S.-born Mexican American female
Consultee ethnicity/gender	European American female	European American female	Mexican born male
Consultant ethnicity/gender	U.S.-born Vietnamese American female	U.S.-born European American (German and Czech) female	U.S.-born Iranian American and Polish American female
Communication style (consultant vs. consultee)	Same: Indirect, indirect	Different: Indirect, direct	Different: Indirect, direct
Teacher languages (native and second)	Bilingual: English and Spanish	Monolingual: English	Bilingual: Spanish and English
Initial client behaviors	Lack of oral participation, shy, behind on major history project	Acting out, peer conflicts, T perceives S as bossy, controlling, manipulating	Low math skills and confidence, relies on adults to initiate math, low self-esteem in social interactions

Consultee outcomes			
Conceptual and behavioral change	Yes	No	Yes
Other	Increases in: attention to cultural and individual differences, knowledge, confidence, and objectivity	T sought counseling for student	Increases in: attention to individual differences within cultural context; expanded teaching approaches
Client outcomes	Exposure to different instructional approaches; improved social interaction, verbal participation in class, and peer relationships	Client received counseling and showed some improvements in peer interactions; student identified by T as Student of the Week	Access to different instructional approaches; increased confidence and skill in basic math facts that T reported extended to other subjects; increased T attention.
Consultant outcomes	Increased confidence, knowledge, learning, skill	Decreased confidence and self-perception of skill; consultant decided to focus more directly on client needs and less on consultee cultural views	Increased confidence, knowledge, learning, skill
Overall consultant perception about consultation success	Successful	Unsuccessful	Successful

Methodological, data, and researcher triangulation were achieved through the use of multiple methods (narrative case studies, matrix methods, and quantitative scales collected at regular intervals) and multiple types of data (formative and summative narrative responses to structured questions, weekly consultation session notes, rating scales, and comprehensive written case analysis) collected by a diverse group of beginning consultants working in different school settings. The consultants, consultees, and clients represent several dimensions of diversity (e.g., age, gender, ethnicity, level of experience) and three of Ingraham's (2000) four consultation constellations (consultant–consultee ethnic similarity, consultant–client similarity, and tri-cultural consultation systems), with both culturally similar and culturally different relationships included. In addition to triangulation, member checks and careful attention to consultant feedback contributed to the study's dependability and confirmability. Numerous member checks between the researcher and the consultants provided additional means to reduce investigator bias, check for information accuracy and representation of consultant constructions, and to explore potential emerging theory and interpretations. Consultants reviewed materials for their own and the other two cases, and their comments and perspectives became part of the final review of the study results and manuscript preparation. Results of within-case and cross-case analyses were included in member checks and are reported later in this article. The member-checking process continued during the development and writing of this report.

THREE CASE SUMMARIES OF MULTICULTURAL CONSULTEE-CENTERED CONSULTATION

This article presents summaries of three cases and analyses of qualitative data, with focus on specific MCCC process and practice issues that emerged. Novice consultants' conceptualizations of their consultations are examined as a means to better understand the choices, representations, and thinking of consultants at regular points in their cases. Each case summary includes description of (a) the members of the consultation system; (b) the point of entry and presenting problem; (c) the consultation process and problem analysis; (d) interventions with students and teachers; (e) outcomes for consultees and clients; and (f) analyses of individual, group, and systemic issues.

Case One[1]: Conceptual Change Through Increasing Cultural Awareness and Perspective of a European American Teacher Toward a Vietnamese American Student

Members of the consultation system. This consultation system involved consultant–client ethnic and linguistic similarity with a culturally different teacher. Both teacher and consultant were bilingual females, in different languages, and the consultant, consultee, and client all shared a preference for an indirect style of communication. A European American[2] experienced teacher (T) in her mid-40s sought consultation regarding a student in her class. T had been teaching in an English immersion class for 3 years where she used her fluent Spanish and English bilingual skills to support student learning. The consultant (C) was a 24-year-old U.S.-born Vietnamese American whose parents had immigrated to the U.S. 1 year before she was born. She grew up in southern California and is bilingual in English and Vietnamese. The student client (S) was a 12-year-old boy who just arrived in the U.S. from Vietnam. The consultation for this case involved six sessions over a 3-month period (with holiday breaks), typically held in the classroom or conference room for about 20 to 25 min per session. The 1,400-student middle school is multiethnic, with about 44% Hispanic and Latino, 27% European American, 19% African American, 5% Filipino, 2% Pacific Islander, and small percentages of Asian American and Native American students. Twenty-four percent of the school's population is composed of English Language Learners, and 43% received free or reduced lunches.

Point of entry and presenting problem. Due to the student's limited proficiency in English, he was placed in an English immersion class (that actually functioned as a Spanish–English bilingual class) in a southern Cali-

---

[1]Lynda Nguyen, the consultant for Case 1, is now a school psychologist in the San Francisco Bay Area. Portions of this case were presented in Ingraham (in press).

[2]The term *European American* is used here, rather than a more specific indication of the ethnic heritage of Caucasians or Whites, (a) when a person uses that term as their ethnic identity, as the consultant did in Case 2, or (b) when the specific ethnic origin is unknown and the consultant infers the consultee's ethnicity as European American, as in Cases 1 and 2. Consultant inference is an incomplete way to establish ethnic identity. Use of an ethnic identity scale, responses to direct questions about consultee ethnic identity, or direct self-identifying statements are preferred and are recommended in future studies.

fornia school. T was concerned about the S's adjustment to her class, stating that he rarely sought help, was quiet and shy in class, and hesitated to speak aloud in English. T was concerned that S had not yet done much work for a major history project. C used MCCC to address the teacher's concerns.

The consultation process and problem analysis.   C reported three aspects of the initial problem situation: (a) T's insecure feelings, need for increased competence in communicating with S, and increased knowledge of S's cultural background; (b) S's advanced skills in math, thus a possible mismatch with his skills and the current level of instruction; and (c) S's incomplete history project. Initially, C was concerned that T "would use me as a crutch in supporting [the student] and therefore would not develop her own skills in working with students of different cultural and linguistic backgrounds."

C initially hypothesized that S's timid and shy behavior in class was culturally based. C knew respect in the Vietnamese culture is shown by listening and being quiet, which is sometimes interpreted by Americans as shyness and timidity. Upon observation in the classroom and additional time in consultation, C revised her initial hypotheses to reflect her awareness that T may need to increase her objectivity and skills as well. C observed T giving oral directions to students first in Spanish, then in English. T referred to several cultural stereotypes, such as S's excellent abilities in math, as related to his ethnicity, but seemed unaware of how his interpersonal style might relate to his culture. T, experienced in Spanish–English bilingual education, did not seem to realize that her teaching methods were not meeting the needs of this Vietnamese American student and possibly the Filipino student also in the classroom who had limited social interactions. C asked questions about the lesson and T's expectations for learning. The lesson was a historical unit that focused on the explorations of the western United States during the 1800's. The classroom activities built on the students' understanding of the era of cowboys, covered wagons, and rustic American history, a history with which this student from Vietnam was very unfamiliar. Because many of T's students were excited about the unit, T did not understand why the referred student was not enthusiastic and participating.

Data collected during the consultation included extensive discourse about T's present knowledge about Vietnamese culture, her current teaching strategies with S, analysis of his classroom work, classroom observations, work samples in math and history, and resources on Vietnamese culture.

Creating conceptual change in the consultee.   C worked first to de-velop T's empathy for S's unique cultural and linguistic background, and his experience as an immigrant to a new continent. She expanded T's frame of reference to better attend to S's perspective, thereby supporting the teacher–student relationship and increased use of instructional methods to meet S's needs. This is where the paradigm shift and conceptual change (Sandoval, in press), or the turning (Hylander, 2000), occurred. Once T un-derstood the experience through the eyes of a newly immigrated English learner surrounded by unfamiliar languages and cultures, a new represen-tation of the student was possible.

Through this intervention, T saw that she needed to use more contex-tual cues, gestures, visual aides, and nonverbal communication tools to support S's understanding of T's instructions. C helped T access her previ-ously learned strategies for supporting second-language development of students. Additionally, T recognized her need for knowledge of S's cul-ture, and she obtained resources about Vietnamese culture such as books, an English–Vietnamese dictionary, and so on, thus diminishing her feel-ings of helplessness and increasing her confidence in her ability to work with S. C used self-disclosure to share her own experiences with learning two languages and with the interface of a Vietnamese home culture and the European American school culture. She provided additional cultural information to help contextualize T's interpretation of S's classroom be-haviors. Then C worked to create better inclusion of S's experiences with the class activities and classmates.

Consultee interventions with the student.   C supported T in imple-menting activities that allowed S to share about his culture, thereby further-ing the cultural learning of T and other students in the class and giving S an opportunity to share his knowledge, rather than his lack of English skills. The students were eager to learn more about S's experiences and culture. T paired S with a classmate with high math skills with whom S was already comfortable, and they worked together as peers.

Outcomes.   Instead of falling victim to T's initial quest for C to inter-vene directly with the student and fix the problem, C used one-downsmanship and MCCC methods (e.g., support consultee and client success) to support T's learning about how to work with S. The teacher greatly expanded her understanding of S's life experiences and culture, other students in the class learned about Vietnamese culture and immigration from a distant continent, and S benefited. In T's comments and C's own classroom observations, S increased his level of interaction and participation, increased his social interactions with peers, and was more comfortable answering questions in English, but not usually in front of the class. He remained timid and rarely sought help, but overall, T reported that S improved. C observed S in class reading aloud from a Vietnamese folklore book written in Vietnamese. S's peers were extremely excited to hear the stories of Vietnamese folklore and were more accepting of S and his culture. C learned that by helping T explore the situation from the perspective of S, much conceptual change could occur.

Analysis of case one: Building consultee perspective, confidence, and knowledge. When C elected to work towards increasing T's capacity to relate to S, rather than using her expertise and cultural understanding to intervene directly with T, positive outcomes resulted for the teacher, student, peers, and consultant. Both consultant and consultee reported that they increased their knowledge, skills, and confidence through working on this case. The consultant's use of one-downsmanship and self-disclosure of her own experience being Vietnamese American helped T see the situation from S's perspective without threatening T's feelings of competence. This shifted the attention from T's feelings of helplessness and cultural incompetence towards increased empathy for S and a focus on his emotional, social, and learning needs. This shift empowered T to access her knowledge and skill for working with English learners, restore her feelings of competence, and engage in some new strategies with S.

Case 2[3]: Challenges of Seeking Conceptual Change in a Teacher Perceived as Adopting a Color-Blind Paradigm by a European American Consultant

Members of the consultation system. This case involved consultant–consultee ethnic similarity and cross-cultural student–consultee and student–consultant relationships. The consultant, consultee, and client were female. The student (S) was a biracial African American and Mexican American female, age 6, who used a direct style of communication with high energy and assertiveness. Her teacher (T), the

---

[3]Carrie Buchek, the consultant for Case 2, is now a school psychologist in the San Diego area.

consultee, requested consultation and described S as an "energy consumer" who had poor peer relationships. C described T as a monolingual European American, in her mid-to-late 30s, who used a direct style of communication, exhibited professionalism, and conveyed a serious demeanor. C, a 24-year-old European American (mostly German and Czech heritage) female raised in Texas, prefers an indirect style of communication. She described her behavior and personality as professional, tentative, and timid in the context of this case. The case involved four 20-min consultation sessions, typically held in the classroom. C had worked at the school for about 6 months and had consulted with T about another student prior to this consultation referral. This school of about 1,000 students has a predominantly Latino population, with 62% designated as English Language Learners. The student body is about 76% Hispanic and Latino, 16% European American, 3% African American, and had small percentages of Asian American, Filipino, Pacific Islander, and Native American students in a lower income (82% of students receive free or reduced lunches) working-class community.

Point of entry.   T referred this case for consultation due to her concern about S's peer relationships and behavior. T described four areas of concern related to S: (a) "She is impulsive," (b) "She is bossy" with peers, (c) "She is manipulative"with peers, and (d) "She struggles with reading." C asked for and received elaboration, descriptions, and examples for each of these concerns. Given the frustration with which T described her concerns and the focus of the examples, C's initial hypothesis was that T greatly disliked S and found S's behaviors and personality unappealing. C noted T's exasperated tone of voice and T's description of S's behaviors with peers as related to negative attributes rather than leadership or other strengths related to similar behaviors. T did not mention S's ethnicity when discussing her concerns.

The consultation process and problem analysis.   When C asked T about the ethnicity of the student, C reported that T replied "Hispanic or something" with a shrug and noncommittal tone. This and other comments by T influenced C's hypothesis development regarding T's need for knowledge and increased objectivity. From C's perspective, the most salient problem in the case was T's color-blind approach in working with culturally diverse students. C had read Ingraham's (2000) description of the color-blind approach when consultees seek to treat all their students the same and ignore student ethnicity, culture, or color. In this approach, a well-meaning person tries to treat all students alike and ignore their cultural or ethnic affiliation. Although proponents of this approach argue that it supports equality in their interactions with others, many feel strongly that it denies or negates one's cultural or ethnic identity, an aspect of one's identity or self-worth that may be highly significant for an individual. C was educated in multicultural counseling, diversity issues, cultural advocacy, and the value of affirming ethnic and cultural identity. She presented at a national conference on the relationship between her own journey in White identity development and her experiences in a multiethnic graduate program. She perceived the T's value system to be very divergent from her own.

C provided examples to support her assessment that T needed further development in her knowledge about ethnic identity and family issues, cross-cultural skills, objectivity, and confidence in how to work with her students. C gave the following account to illustrate why she believed T's color-blind paradigm showed that T was lacking objectivity:

> I came in wanting to open the dialogue about her as a White woman teaching students of color. I wanted to put her in the expert role to allow her to feel comfortable talking about these issues. So I started the session with a statement and question similar to the following: "When I walked into your room the other day, I noticed that your class is predominantly Mexican American and other students of color, and I am interested in hearing what that has been like for you. You must have a lot of experience with this population." Her response was to confidently and proudly tell me that the key is to treat them all the same and that she tries to leave all the colors outside the door so that she can come in open-minded and treating them equally. She mentioned that was what she learned in school and has found it to be the best policy. This comment threw me off because I wasn't expecting to hear it again and didn't prepare enough to respond—so I didn't, and then she cornered me with, "Don't you agree, isn't that the best way to teach them—I think that's the best thing for you to learn as a student—to treat everybody equally." I froze and changed the subject to [the student].

At that point in the case, C felt she was completely blocking and had no idea how to approach this issue with T. C decided to meet with a trusted peer about the case for feedback and perspective.

Data collected during the consultation process included discussions throughout the consultation sessions, review of school records, and information gathered by C. C had attended a team meeting about S's brother, thus she had information about the home environment from her team meeting notes. She also talked with the school counselor to inquire about the family and ask if there was additional information she should know.

Interventions with the teacher.   The consultant continued consultation with T in an attempt to co-construct a shared analysis of the problem. She tried to use mental health consultation approaches with a goal of increasing T's cultural knowledge and empathy for working with S. Perhaps a difficulty here is that T and C did not share the same analysis of the problem. In the next session, following feedback from her peer, C shifted the consultation discourse to issues of identity development, S's home life, and S's family experiences as context for the classroom behaviors. C tried asking questions to open T's thinking to how S might be feeling, but T did not respond. C reported that T's comment was something like "Yeah, I've heard her story. She, like a lot of us, has had a tough life." Trying to invite T's empathy towards S, C reflected to T, "It must be confusing for her being both Black and Mexican—especially as it seems like she doesn't have any African American role models around." C observed T not responding verbally and staring blankly. Consistent with Caplan's mental health model (Caplan & Caplan, 1993), C shared a parable about a biracial friend who struggled with ethnic identity issues, trying to take the focus off the present interpersonal relationships and provide a little distance. C disclosed that her friend felt incomplete until she took it upon herself to seek out information about the culture she didn't know. C reported that T listened but appeared uncomfortable and with closed body language. Feeling unproductive with her efforts to open T to S's perspective, C refocused on T's goal for S. T expressed a desire to find ways for S to interact with her peers more positively. T said she'd like to see S develop more confidence, security in her skills, and more consistency in her interactions with her friends. C asked how she thought T could give her those things. T quietly stated, "I don't know."

Outcomes.   C began providing counseling services to S to support her development of self-confidence and positive peer relationships, and C consulted with T to share observations and topics learned through counseling. C found S to be very talented. C shared information about S's strengths with T and tried to affect the teacher–student relationship by helping T to see and support S's positive behaviors and attributes. T selected S to be Student of the Week. When C asked T about this award, T responded that S is capable of having a really good week and getting along with everyone and that she had no idea of what made this week go so well for S. Following the conclusion of the case, C reported that T began to see S slightly more positively and that T appeared to listen more openly to C. From this case, C learned to be very cautious about raising cultural issues directly with a teacher unless she has an early indication that the teacher is open to exploring cultural issues. Instead, C began to deal with cultural themes more indirectly by focusing on student behavior and learning.

Analysis of individual, group, and systemic issues.   T believed S was the problem and was unresponsive to C's attempts to help her develop psychological mindedness and understand the context for S's behaviors. Despite her attempts, C was unsuccessful in finding an opening to reframe T's conceptualization of the problem. Similarly, she was unsuccessful in supporting T in recognizing that T's approach and perception were part of the problem. C was determined to explore cultural issues in the consultation in her attempt to intervene on T's color-blind perspective, but she had difficulty finding a topic on which to share understanding and co-construction with T. C tried to persist with her agenda in a more indirect mode, consistent with her communication style, and was paralyzed when T confronted her and asked C for agreement on T's color-blind paradigm. Co-construction of the problem identification and analysis did not occur. While C and T share the same ethnicity, their ages and communication styles were different. Both C and T seemed unable to shift from their initial hypothesis about the problem definition into a shared understanding of the problem and the goals. Unlike the situation between the Vietnamese American consultant and European American teacher in Case 1, in this case, both C and T were European Americans. T, confident in her years of experience, did not see a need to learn more about S's culture or home situation and was not open to exploring issues of culture and contextual factors.

Case 3[4]: Conceptual Change Through a Focus on Instructional Processes and Individual Learning Style With a Mexican American Teacher and Student With a Multicultural Female Consultant

Members of the consultation system.   This case represented consultee–client similarity in ethnicity and culture of origin, and a cross-gender, cross-cultural consultant–consultee relationship. S was a 10-year-old Mexican American female who was described as quiet and trying hard in school. S responded well to teacher encouragement, and she

---

[4]Rosalyn Afshani, the consultant for Case 3, is now a school psychologist in the San Diego City School District.

enjoyed helping in the class, though she relied on T for assistance. T referred S to the school's Student Study Team for group problem-solving. C met with T after the group meeting and offered individual consultation, which T accepted. According to C, T was a first generation Mexican American male in his early 40s who was an experienced elementary school teacher. He used a direct style of communication, showing little emotion or frustration, and had a firm approach to teaching in his class; his students were well behaved. He was organized, friendly, kind, and accessible to his students. He taught in an English Language Development class for students learning English whose native language is not English, incorporating Spanish into his teaching. C was a 26-year-old U.S.-born female with multicultural heritage. Born and raised in Buffalo, New York, she is of Iranian American and Polish American descent; prefers an indirect style of communication that involves non-threatening, gentle, and caring expressions; and described her personality as talkative and usually happy, sometimes feeling intimidation and challenged self-esteem when working with authoritative figures. The school is in a predominantly Latino community with 45% of the students Spanish-speaking English Language Learners, and both English and Spanish are spoken at school. Five consultation sessions, typically 25 to 35 min in duration, were held in T's classroom over a 3-month period.

Point of entry.   T referred this case due to his concern about S's low academic skills in math and S's tendency to rely on adults before initiating math assignments, even when the task was within her instructional range. Additionally, T was concerned about S's low level of confidence in math and low self-esteem regarding social interactions. While S was kind and interacted with peers, she rarely initiated peer relationships and spent most of her time with another passive student.

The consultation process and problem analysis.   Based on T's comments and concerns, C believed T didn't understand why S was having difficulty. C initially hypothesized a mismatch between the instructional method and S's learning style. In their first consultation session, C and T focused on the curricular expectations for fifth grade math, specific approaches to achieve these expectations, and S's needs as a learner. C used collaborative instructional consultation methods to engage in task analysis, error analysis, and analysis of the instructional delivery approach and S's learning style. C observed during math instruction, and T and C reviewed S's work samples.

Initially, C felt a power difference between herself and T, primarily relating to their differences in gender, age, culture, and language, and she was somewhat intimidated by what she perceived to be T's serious nature. C felt uncomfortable when, in their first session, T asked C if she spoke Spanish; she does not. C was concerned that this might cause a barrier in their rapport and communication. C tried to develop empathy and establish a bridge of understanding by talking about her own multicultural background and her awareness of what it is like living outside the dominant U.S. culture. She established rapport and used an indirect form of one-downsmanship by taking on the role of cultural learner, asking T about bilingual education, and about Mexican cultural values and beliefs. C used self-disclosure, sharing her own experiences as a bicultural woman living 3,000 miles from her hometown, and she helped create emotional safety by showing empathy for the difficulties presented to English Language Learners.

Data collected during consultation included a review of the cumulative folder (with support from an interpreter to help translate the Spanish content), classroom instructional observation, review of work samples, and discussion in consultation of the instructional process.

Interventions with the teacher and consultant.   Through the consultation process, both T and C learned and developed. C used concepts and techniques from instructional consultation to enhance T's conceptualization of the problem, and mental health techniques to put T in an expert role and support his desire to be knowledgeable and educational. C adopted a learner mode regarding the culture of T and S, and worked towards helping T recognize S's individuality and learning style. Through use of one-downsmanship and her openness and expressed desire to learn about areas of T's expertise (e.g., culture and second-language instruction), C modeled a professional learning style that was both educated and receptive to new learning, a style she hoped to support in T. She sought out literature on working with Hispanic students and families in an educational context. She combined this approach with her use of instructional consultation methodology to explore specific aspects of the curriculum with T, S's current level of skills and style of learning, and the methods of instructional delivery. They agreed that S was having difficulty organizing her numbers with specific operations. They discussed possible interventions together, including the use of flash cards for math facts, graph paper to align numbers, and samples (that S could keep on her desk) of the steps involved in the math procedures. They talked about ways to do one problem together to ensure that S understood the directions and then to encourage S to work independently. Also, T made adjustments in the assignment length and how he gave instructions.

Outcomes.   C observed greater specificity in T's ability to examine details related to the teaching–learning process, to answer focused questions, and to collect relevant information. Brainstorming produced possible interventions from which T could choose and implement. He felt successful in finding ways to more effectively teach S and in supporting C's learning about his culture and educational expertise. In the follow-up debriefings with the researcher, C reflected:

> Although she still struggled in math, she showed increased success with basic math facts using flash cards. She was better able to complete computations using graph paper...Also, I recall that the Step Cards that she taped to her desk were helpful, although she still needed teacher assistance for clarity. As her ability to recall the steps improved, she displayed more confidence and would often show her teacher her work (for approval at first, then with more confidence). Her skills in reading the language-loaded problems did not improve ... but that was not our primary focus at that time .... In addition to just improving some basic skills, I feel that her confidence improved because she was receiving much needed individual attention from the Basic Skills teacher, the aide, and her regular teacher.

T reported that S developed a sense of competence, increasing her motivation to learn, and this spread across all areas of learning. C felt successful in helping T to develop and expand his definition of the problem, to ultimately examine how his instructional processes were a factor, and to adjust his instruction to better meet the student's needs. At the end of the case, C reflected that her work with T "has brought new meaning to the consultation process for me, and I am more confident in working with consultees whose ethnic identity is different from my own." Both T and C improved their skills in task and error analysis for math. The student benefited by increasing her math skills, academic motivation, and perceived competence.

Analysis of individual, group and systemic issues.   Initially C felt uneasiness pertaining to her age, gender, and culture in relation to T, and this increased her self-consciousness and challenged her confidence. Thus, she used one-downsmanship and approaches that served to support T's feelings of competence and ownership of the intervention and techniques that matched his style and desires. The cultural context for this case, in a predominantly Latino community with the consultant-trainee working under the supervision of a Latina supervisor, further challenged C's confidence and contextual grounding. C succeeded in creating a bridge between herself and T so that she could influence the development of conceptual change. She drew upon her experiences as a teacher, understanding of the intersection of culture and individual differences, and as a bicultural person living far from her hometown. She demonstrated her openness and desire for learning from T more about the Mexican culture and second-language instructional processes. This created emotional safety for T to share his expertise and remain receptive to C's questions regarding the specific learning style of S. C helped reinforce T's cultural expertise while attempting to deconstruct his understanding of this student, based primarily in his own learning style and culture, to create better balance in the problem-identification between the influences of cultural and individual differences. C thereby helped enhance T's knowledge, skill, and objectivity and restore his confidence; and, at the same time, greatly increased her own knowledge, skill, objectivity, and confidence regarding the process of multicultural consultation.

ANALYSIS AND INTERPRETATION OF CASES

The findings identify some of the conditions whereby consultants were successful and unsuccessful in working with consultees to develop new conceptualizations through MCCC. Each case demonstrates MCCC in action, and the cases are rich with consultant perceptions of a how a wide range of factors are associated with the specific processes and outcomes. Table 2 summarizes some of the key ways the cases were different. The results demonstrate that in some cases (e.g., Cases 1 and 3), even novice consultants can successfully raise cultural hypotheses with experienced teacher consultees and co-construct case conceptualizations that lead to positive interventions. All three cases involved beginning consultants, unsure of their skills in consultation, who were working over 4 to 6 consultation sessions with experienced teachers 10 to 20 years their senior.

The cases also reveal some of the challenges consultants face when working with teachers who have defined attitudes and attributions about the progress of their culturally diverse students. In Case 2, the consultant perceived the consultee as adopting a color-blind paradigm (a worldview in contrast with the consultant's), and had difficulty finding a way to support consultee conceptual change. Although she used some of the approaches of classic mental health consultation (e.g., Caplan & Caplan, 1993), such as parables, one-downsmanship, focusing on others rather than directly on the consultee, and seeking consultee empathy for the perspective of the client, these were insufficient to co-construct a new conceptualization with the consultee. One possible reason may involve the consultee's perception of the consultant's knowledge in areas relevant for the case. In Case 2, the consultant and consultee were both European American monolingual females, and perhaps the consultee did not perceive the consultant as having cultural expertise that might inform the consultee's work with this African American and Mexican American student.

When looking across the cases for common themes and patterns, the complexities of ways that culture can influence consultation are apparent. The findings of this study suggest that factors such as the focus of consultation (e.g., instructional and mental health vs. behavioral and mental health), methods of bridging across diversity, teacher attitudes toward a target student, and consultant success in bringing up cultural issues may be related to success or failure in co-constructing the problem definition and eventual success of interventions and consultant self-perceptions.

The matrix comparisons across cases revealed both similarities and differences in specific MCCC and traditional consultation approaches used. All three consultants used one-downsmanship, invited the consultee to adopt a psychological mindedness and empathy for the client, and sought feedback from others. The difference was that consultants in Cases 1 and 3 also used other MCCC approaches including self-disclosure regarding the consultant's own cultural learning process, reframing, bridging across differences, creating emotional safety, co-constructing the problem definition, and reframing cultural perspectives, whereas the consultant in Case 2 did not. Additionally, the consultant was the primary person to deliver the interventions in Case 2, whereas the consultees in Cases 1 and 3 had primary responsibility for interventions. See Table 2 for examples of other differences.

Co-Construction of Case Conceptualization

The results of the qualitative analyses suggest that when the co-construction of the case conceptualization did not occur, new concepts were not formed, and the intervention was unsuccessful. In other cases seen in Ingraham's consultation course and in Case 2 reported here, the consultants did not know how to bring up potential consultee cultural bias and avoided this issue in the sessions. In these cases, new conceptualizations were not constructed between the consultant and consultee, and the consultants developed self-perceptions of low multicultural consultation skill and confidence. Moreover, without the co-construction of the problem definition, the development of interventions was compromised, limiting consultee and client outcomes. In Cases 1 and 3, the consultants were successful in raising discussion of multicultural issues between the consultee and client in ways that contributed to the co-construction of a new conceptualization of the problem and subsequent interventions.

Themes in Successful Versus Unsuccessful Consultation Cases

What factors seem to account for the successful versus unsuccessful attempts at co-constructing conceptual change? There were a variety of patterns that characterized the successful versus unsuccessful consultation cases, including differences in the nature of the student behaviors, ethnicities of the student clients, teacher attitudes towards the students, consultant use of self-disclosure, cultural identity of the consultants, focus of consultation, consultee willingness to explore modifications in their instructional approaches, and area of specialization of consultees. Because of the variation in naturally occurring cross-cultural consultation cases, it is not possible to isolate each of these differences in the cases and determine their relative contribution towards the case outcomes. This would be more of a positivistic paradigm and would require a much larger number of case studies than was available for the present study.

It is possible to raise hypotheses about potential contributing factors and, through the member-checking processes with the consultants and triangulation with the various sources of data within and across cases, to assess the relative merit of each hypothesis. There are several potential explanations for the differences in the successful and unsuccessful cases. For example, contextual and power influences between consultants and consultees were salient in the differences between successful and unsuccessful co-constructions of problem definition, with the consultant–consultee similarity (Case 2) as the most challenging for the novice consultant to raise cultural hypotheses with the experienced consultee.

Perhaps teachers perceived the consultees who were culturally different from themselves (Cases 1 and 3) as having expertise relevant to the consultee's conceptualization of the case, whereas this was not the case for the unsuccessful consultation case.

The consultants who were successful in supporting consultee conceptual change used self-disclosure of their own learning process to bridge with the consultees, but the unsuccessful consultant did not. Interestingly, both cases where consultants used self-disclosure, rapport and problem-solving (Cases 1 and 3) were more effective than the case without self-disclosure. Self-disclosure may serve to support simultaneously the goals of using one-downsmanship, as recommended by Caplan and Caplan (1993), to reduce the interpersonal power of the consultant, as well as two approaches recommended in Ingraham (2000): (a) creating an emotionally safe environment within which to discuss cultural issues; and (b) normalizing and modeling the vulnerability of cultural learning.

An additional hypothesis has to do with the consultee's bilingual skills and values about cultural differences. The two teachers who successfully adopted a conceptual change were both bilingual teachers (Cases 1 and 3) trained in second-language acquisition who had been raised in or who had traveled to Mexico. One was bilingual and bicultural, and one was bilingual but not bicultural. They were more receptive to a perspective that valued cultural identity and heritage as integral to one's being, however the monolingual teacher for whom conceptual change was not successful did not share these perspectives. This made it much more difficult for the consultant to find a bridge to reframe and co-construct the conceptualization of the problem. It was challenging to raise cultural hypotheses with this teacher because cultural influences were not within the teacher's value system. It appears that the consultees were in very different stages of ethnic identity development, although no measure was used to assess this construct.

Certain threats to objectivity may be more resistant to conceptual change than others. The color-blind paradigm of the teacher in Case 2 may have been more resistant to change than the paradigms of overlooking individual differences in learning style (Case 3) or language and culture of origin (Case 1). Creating conceptual change regarding the color-blind paradigm involved attitude change with respect to an approach the consultee thought was correct. In contrast, in Cases 1 and 3, reframing and sharing different interpretations for the presenting problems were sufficient to move towards conceptual change and successful co-construction of the case. The consultants were not proposing an interpretation that was in direct opposition to the consultee's, as in Case 2.

Another potential pattern involved the focus of the consultation and the success in co-constructing problem conceptualizations. The two cases that focused on the instructional process (Cases 1 and 3) involved greater levels of co-constructed problem definitions and improved student and consultee outcomes, but the case that focused on modifying the teacher's conceptualization, student behavior, and consultee stress reduction was less successful (Case 2). Cases 1 and 3 combined instructional consultation with MCCC, thereby providing greater focus on the student and the learning process than the focus on teacher attitudes addressed primarily through mental health consultation, as seen in Case 2. Perhaps when the consultant seeks to address color-blindness, greater time is needed to establish rapport, consultant credibility, and initial intervention successes in areas the consultee identifies as the presenting problem, before the teacher is willing to consider cultural components of the problem definition.

When the consultant and consultee are of the same ethnicity but different ages and levels of professional experience, as seen in Case 2, the power differentials may compromise the consultant's referent power to influence conceptual change and reframing. This same dynamic was seen in other cases among Ingraham's students where novice European American consultants were working with experienced European American consultees when the consultant hypothesized cultural theme interference on the part of the consultee. During one of the member-checking phases of this study, the consultant from Case 2 reflected that now, 18 months after the case, she finds that it is easier to raise cultural hypotheses with teachers who are ethnically different from her than with same-ethnicity consultees. In the interview with Ingraham, the consultant agreed that it is plausible because she thinks culturally different consultees may be more open to discussing cultural issues than their European American counterparts. She said that she was (and still is) scared of self-disclosure for fear of insulting European American teachers (and even friends) who may be in a different stage of identity development. She observed that unless a European American teacher makes a suggestion to lead her to believe the teacher is open to exploring cultural themes, she is cautious and prefers to take a very indirect route to raising these issues, if at all. She explained, "I struggle with how to help target the stage [of identity development] they're in and [how to] raise their consciousness to bring it to next level—certainly this is a sticky arena."

DISCUSSION

The findings are discussed in relation to the multicultural consultation framework (Ingraham, 2000) with implications for future research and practice. The study suggests that bicultural and multicultural novice consultants can succeed in raising cultural issues with experienced teachers through multicultural consultation. One implication is that attention to the components the framework—called *power differentials* and *strategies to support cultural learning*—may be critical for success in MCCC. Both cases with positive consultee outcomes (Cases 1 and 3) involved several aspects of framing the problem and using multicultural consultation strategies, whereas the consultant in the unsuccessful case (Case 2) recognized, retrospectively, that she had not developed these.

Another implication is that greater focus is needed on novice European American consultants working on behalf of culturally diverse students with experienced European American consultees to support consultants in raising cultural issues in ways that lead to positive co-constructions of the problem. Pope-David, Reynolds, Dings, and Nielson (1995) found that self-perceived multicultural counseling competencies were greater for graduate students of color than their White peers, possibly related to their different levels of experience with multicultural issues. Tarver Behring et al. (2000) found that the European American novice consultants were less likely to use culturally based adjustments to traditional consultation models than the consultants of color. The European American consultants sometimes raised cultural hypotheses but did not know how to adapt the interventions to provide culturally compatible adjustments and interventions. This pattern may have existed in the present cases as well. Given the challenges that European American novice consultants face when working with experienced European American consultees, they may need additional support and coaching in methods to foster conceptual change. In this study, the consultant in Case 2, unlike the consultants in Cases 1 and 3, did not access the consultation professor's or seminar's coaching specifically for this case, thus it is not known if coaching would have affected the case's processes or outcomes.

Given the results of this study, future research is recommended to explore the features of the consultation constellation (e.g., consultee characteristics and training, consultant ethnicity and biculturalism) and the consultant approaches (e.g., self-disclosure, co-construction, building bridges) that are central to the outcomes of MCCC. With the naturalistic nature of this inquiry, determinations of causality are not the goal. Controlling for all possible differences between the consultants and consultees in the study was not the intention of this research, thus some of the differences between the cases confound variables that may be influential in the consultation outcomes. In all cases, the consultants were female, second-year graduate students, who had engaged in exploration and articulation of their own culture and its impact on their consultation. They were several years younger than their experienced teacher consultees. Each consultant conceptualized cultural hypotheses regarding their definition of the problem, sought conceptual change in the consultee, and used consultation strategies to encourage the consultee to explore the influence of culture on the teacher's work with a specific student.

A naturalistic study using case study methods, such as this one, has several limitations. A naturalistic study is not able to control for all competing factors that may influence the outcomes. In this study, two of the consultees happened to be bilingual teachers, and it is not known if monolingual teachers would have shared as readily in the co-construction of a culturally grounded problem definition. The total number of cases is small, thus it is not possible to determine if the findings are due to specific characteristics of these cases or patterns found among many different types of consultation cases. The study was designed to include two European American consultants; however, one of the consultants declined to participate in the qualitative parts of this research, thus attributions to cultural features of European American consultants as opposed to consultants with mixed cultural heritage are unsupportable in the present study. Another limitation involves the focus on consultant perceptions and reports, initially documented while in a graded course, without direct data about consultee or client perceptions. Ideally, consultees would participate in focus groups or member-checking procedures to triangulate the observations and interpretations made by consultants. Additionally, it would be helpful to have a measure of cultural identity development on consultants and consultees. Finally, an external audit, as recommended by qualitative researchers (Erlandson, et al, 1993; Lincoln & Guba, 1985; Miles & Huberman, 1984) was not conducted. While the consultants served as quasi-auditors for each other's cases (case summaries, researcher interpretations, and analyses were sent for review to all three consultants), credibility of the study would be strengthened by formal use of auditors external to the study.

One purpose of a naturalistic qualitative study is to identify avenues for future research. This study points to several directions for future research to investigate the processes and relationships among members of the consultation system, the conceptualizations of consultants and consultees, and their influence on consultation outcomes. Studies with consultants and consultees of different ethnicities, stages of ethnic identity, levels of experience, linguistic competence, values, and gender are needed to better understand the ways each of these relates to consultation outcomes. For example: What is the relationship between the consultant and consultee ethnicity and its influence on consultation processes and outcomes? Do European American versus consultants of ethnically and linguistically diverse backgrounds encounter different reactions from consultees when they raise cultural hypotheses about the problem definition? Is there a difference in willingness to explore cultural hypotheses through consultation among bilingual teachers compared with monolingual English speakers? When consultees have similar cultural and linguistic backgrounds, are there differences in the success of monocultural versus bicultural or multicultural consultants?

Similarly, studies using different consultation models and different multicultural consultation techniques to explore cultural hypotheses are needed to more fully understand potential patterns with one model over another. Specifically, does consultant self-disclosure during consultation affect the consultee's willingness to explore cultural hypotheses associated with problem definition? Which consultant approaches to support consultee's cultural learning in Ingraham's (2000) framework are most linked with consultant success? When working across cultures, what factors are associated with co-construction of the problem definition? Is there a difference in consultant success when consultants focus on the consultee's cultural attitudes versus focusing more on the instructional process? Does instructional consultation, paired with mental health consultation, result in more successful consultation about cultural issues than mental health paired with behavioral or mental health approaches alone?

Finally, research is needed to examine the education and development of consultants and consultees. What kinds of training and support do European American consultants need to effectively raise cultural hypotheses with their senior European American consultees? When consultees demonstrate a belief in a color-blind paradigm, how can consultants best explore cultural views and perspectives? What issues do seasoned European American consultants experience in raising cultural hypotheses with European American consultees?

Raising cultural hypotheses with consultees is complex and challenging. This study explores the perceptions and experiences of three novice consultants who attempted to modify consultee conceptualizations. Their consultees represented different worldviews, values, and competencies.

The findings of this study suggest the possibility that consultants who use self-disclosure of their own cultural learning process and methods to bridge across their differences with consultees may experience greater success in consultation outcomes for all members of the consultation system. Additionally, consultants who combine aspects of instructional and mental health consultation may be more successful in modifying teacher behaviors and conceptualizations than those who focus primarily on teacher attitudes, behaviors, and beliefs. Further research on successful and unsuccessful consultation cases that target consultee cultural conceptualizations is needed to support these tentative findings.

ACKNOWLEDGMENTS

Colette L. Ingraham greatly appreciates the generous contributions of Rosalyn Afshani, Carrie Buchek, and Lynda Nguyen, who were second-year graduate students in my consultation course at the time they conducted the consultation cases reported here. Each, now a successful school psychologist in a multicultural school district, has helped further my own learning, and has graciously given permission to include her reflections and experiences here.

REFERENCES

Brown, D. (1997). Implications of cultural values for cross-cultural consultation with families. *Journal of Counseling and Development, 76,* 29–35.

Caplan, G., & Caplan, R. B. (1993). *Mental health consultation and collaboration.* San Francisco: Jossey-Bass.

Creswell, J. W. (1994). *Research design: Qualitative and quantitative approaches.* Thousand Oaks, CA: Sage.

Duncan, C., & Pryzwansky, W. B. (1993). Effects of race, racial identity development, and orientation style on perceived consultant effectiveness. *Journal of Multicultural Counseling and Development, 21,* 88–96.

Erlandson, D. A., Harris, E. L., Skipper, B. L., & Allen, S. D. (1993). *Doing naturalistic inquiry: A guide to methods.* Newbury Park, CA: Sage.

Gibbs, J. T. (1980). The interpersonal orientation in mental health: Toward a mode of ethnic variations in consultation. *Journal of Community Psychology, 8,* 195–207.

Harris, K. C. (1991). An expanded view on consultation competencies for educators serving culturally and linguistically diverse exceptional students. *Teacher Education and Special Education, 14*(1), 25–29.

Harris, K. C. (1996). Collaboration within a multicultural society. *Remedial and Special Education, 17,* 2–10.

Henning-Stout, M. (1994). Thoughts on being a White consultant. *Journal of Educational and Psychological Consultation, 5,* 269–273.

Hylander, I. (2000). *Turning processes: The changing representations in consultee-centered case consultation* (Linköping Studies in Education and Psychology No. 74). Linköping, Sweden: Linköping University, Department of Behavioral Sciences.

Ingraham, C. L. (2000). Consultation through a multicultural lens: Multicultural and cross-cultural consultation in schools. *School Psychology Review, 29,* 320–343.

Ingraham, C. L. (2002, February). *Multicultural consultation in schools to support teacher and sudent success.* Invited workshop at the annual meeting of the National Association of school Psychologists, Chicago, IL. Audiotapes available (# WS 16) from NASP and Gaylor MultiMedia, Inc.

Ingraham, C. L. (in press). Multicultural consultation: A model for supporting consultees in the development of cultural competence. In N. M. Lambert, I. Hylander, & J. Sandoval (Eds.), *Consultee centered consultation: Improving the quality of professional services in schools and community organizations.* Mahwah, NJ: Lawrence Erlbaum Associates, Inc.

Ingraham, C. L., & Meyers, J. (2000). Introduction to multicultural and cross-cultural consultation in schools: Cultural diversity issues in school consultation. *School Psychology Review, 29,* 315–319.

Ingraham, C. L., & Tarver Behring, S. (1998, August). *Multicultural consultation with diverse parent and teacher consultees: An analysis.* Paper presented at the annual meeting of the American Psychological Association, San Francisco, CA.

Lincoln, Y. S., & Guba, E. G. (1985). *Naturalistic inquiry.* Beverly Hills, CA: Sage.

Lopez, E. (2000). Conducting consultation through interpreters. *School Psychology Review, 29,* 378–388.

Maital, S. L. (2000). Reciprocal distancing: A systems model of interpersonal processes in cross-cultural consultation. *School Psychology Review, 29,* 389–400.

Maxwell, J. A. (1996). *Qualitative research design: An interactive approach* (Applied Social Research Methods Series, No. 41). Thousand Oaks, CA: Sage.

Miles, M. B., & Huberman, A. M. (1984). *Qualitative data analysis: A sourcebook of new method.* Beverly Hills, CA: Sage.

Nastasi, B., Vargas, K., Berstein, R., & Jayasena, A. (2000). Conducting participatory culture-specific consultation: A global perspective on multicultural consultation. *School Psychology Review, 29,* 401–413.

Naumann, W. C., Gutkin, T. B., & Sandoval, S. R. (1996). The impact of consultant race and student race on perceptions of consultant effectiveness and intervention acceptability. *Journal of Educational and Psychological Consultation, 7,* 151–160.

Pinto, R. F. (1981). Consultant orientations and client system perceptions: Styles of cross-cultural consultation. In R. Lippitt & G. L. Lippitt (Eds.), *Systems thinking: A resource for organizational diagnosis and intervention* (pp. 57–74). Washington, DC: International Consultants.

Ponterotto, J. G., (2002). Qualitative research methods: The fifth force in psychology. *The Counseling Psychologist, 30,* 394–406.

Pope-Davis, D. B., Reynolds, A. L., Dings, J. G., & Nielson, D. (1995). Examining multicultural counseling competencies of graduate students in psychology. *Professional Psychology: Research and Practice, 26,* 322–329.

Pope-Davis, D. B., Toporek, R. L., Ortega-Villalobos, L., Lingiéro, D. P., Brittan-Powell, C. S., Liu, W. M., Bashshur, M. R., Codrington, J. N., & Liang, C. T. H. (2002). Client perspectives of multicultural counseling competence: A qualitative examination. *The Counseling Psychologist, 30,* 355–393.

Ramirez, S. Z., Lepage, K. M., Kratochwill, T. R., & Duffy, J. L. (1998). Multicultural issues in school-based consultation: Conceptual and research considerations. *Journal of School Psychology, 36,* 479–509.

Rogers, M. R. (1998). The influence of race and consultant verbal behavior on perceptions of consultant competence and multicultural sensitivity. *School Psychology Quarterly, 13,* 265–280.

Rogers, M. R. (2000). Examining the cultural context of consultation. *School Psychology Review, 29*, 414–18.

Rogers, M. R., Ingraham, C. L., Bursztyn, A., Cajigas-Segredo, N., Esquivel, G., Hess, R., Lopez, E C., & Nahari, S. G. (1999). Providing psychological services to racially, ethnically, culturally, and linguistically diverse individuals in the schools: Recommendations for practice. *School Psychology International Journal, 20,* 243–264.

Sandoval, J. (2001, August). Conceptual change in consultee-centered consultation. In *Explorations in process in practice.* (Seminar proceedings). San Francisco: 3rd International Seminar on Consultee-Centered Consultation.

Sandoval, J. (in press). Conceptual change in consultee-centered consultation. In N. M. Lambert, I. Hylander, & J. Sandoval (Eds.), *Consultee centered consultation: Improving the quality of professional services in schools and community organizations.* Mahwah, NJ: Lawrence Erlbaum Associates, Inc.

Scholz, R. W., & Tietje, O. (2002). *Embedded case study methods: Integrating quantitative and qualitative knowledge.* Thousand Oaks, CA: Sage.

Soo-Hoo, T. (1998). Applying frame of reference and reframing techniques to improve school consultation in multicultural settings. *Journal of Psychological and Educational Consultation, 9,* 325–345.

Sue, D. W. (2001). Multidimensional facets of cultural competence. *The Counseling Psychologist, 29,* 790–821.

Sue, D. W., Ivey, A. E., & Pedersen, P. B. (Eds.). (1996). *A theory of multicultural counseling and therapy.* San Francisco: Brooks/Cole.

Sue, S. (1999). Science, ethnicity, and bias: Where have we gone wrong? *American Psychologist, 54,* 1070–1077.

Tarver Behring, S., Cabello, B., Kushida, D., & Murguia, A (2000). Cultural modifications to current school-based consultation approaches reported by culturally diverse beginning consultants. *School Psychology Review, 29,* 354–367.

Tarver Behring, S., & Ingraham, C. L. (1998). Culture as a central component of consultation: A call to the field. *Journal of Educational and Psychological Consultation, 9,* 57–72.

Wampold, B. E., Licktenberg, J. W., & Waehler, C. A. (2002). Principles of empirically supported interventions in counseling psychology. *The Counseling Psychologist, 30,* 197–217.

Yin, R. K. (1998). The abridged version of case study research: Design and method. In Bickman, L. & Rog, D. J. (Eds.), *Handbook of applied social research methods* (pp. 229–259). Thousand Oaks, CA: Sage.

Colette L. Ingraham, is a Professor in the Department of Counseling and School Psychology at San Diego State University, California. Her experience in multicultural communities as a school-based consultant, researcher, and teacher and supervisor of consultants informs her work. Her interests include multicultural, cross-cultural, and systems perspectives in consultation, intervention, and program development and evaluation.

JOURNAL OF EDUCATIONAL AND PSYCHOLOGICAL CONSULTATION, 14(3&4), 363–368

COMMENTARY

Finally, a Contemporary Treatment of Consultee-Centered Consultation

Walter B. Pryzwansky

University of North Carolina at Chapel Hill

The consultation literature has been challenged by the absence of a typology or classification system. Descriptors such as content (e.g., mental health, behavioral, ecological), focus (e.g., individual, group, systems), and intent (e.g., expert, process, collaborator) could be starting points in such discussions; however, they have not been addressed systematically in the plethora of writings that have mushroomed since Caplan's book (Caplan, 1970). In fact, Caplan did differentiate consultation from several other helping approaches such as supervision and collaboration. But, the seduction of the term, or the prestige associated with the term for the practitioner and academic, was too much to resist using in its more common form. Subsequently, the terms *consultation* and later *collaboration* have found widespread use in society as a whole. As a result, we soon experienced such assertions as the supervisor who preferred to "consult" with his or her supervisee, or the consultant who "collaborated" with the consultee, or the husband who "consults" with his wife about what tie to wear. Yet, the professional definition of these terms is critical to establish for two reasons: (a) interpretable, replicated research is more likely to be generated; and (b) the practitioner can accurately evaluate the process and outcome of his or her work using definitions established for professional use. Thus, the guest editors of this special issue have presented a collection of very important articles to specify clearly what is meant by consultee-centered consultation (a

Correspondence should be addressed to Walter B. Pryzwansky, University of North Carolina at Chapel Hill, CB #3500, 112 Peabody Hall, Chapel Hill, NC 27514. E-mail: waltbp@email.unc.edu

richer descriptor than mental health consultation) in a constructive manner rather than using the red herring type arguments that have come to typify many contemporary model presentations. Also critical to their presentation is the inclusion of the important premises on which the model is based. All too often, such information is missing or forgotten in the literature, and even in preservice training. Finally, tying the descriptions to the internal professional in an organization advances our thinking about consultation practice, since this variable is indeed so critical to the consultation practice found in schools. There are greater contextual constraints for the consultant who is internal to an organization than for the consultant who is external, as was the case in the mental health consultation book on which much of that model was based (Caplan, 1970). For example, consider the "take it or leave it" condition extended to the consultee in the mental health consultation model; this is a formidable tenet to implement, if not possibly an unethical position for the internally based professional to promote.

Sandoval (this issue) extends the conceptual clarification of the consultee-centered model in his article. His principle of beginning the consultation with an examination of what the consultee understands about the problem is critical. This Rashomon approach is hard enough to appreciate, let alone implement. The dynamics of the consultee asking for help are equally challenging to deal with during the entry stage. Consultants need to be sensitive to this element and its influence on the consultee's approach to consultation. Next, the problem-solving steps described by Sandoval follow this complete telling of the story by the consultee (a task made easier if he or she is anxious, frustrated, or mad). The steps require adroit questioning, even more so if the consultee is not particularly driven to seek consultation. The steps of problem-solving that are presented can be of enormous help to the novice consultant. However, he or she cannot lose sight of the importance of the perceptions of the consultee to the first goal of problem-solving, that of problem-finding.

Similarly, in the literature and in training, the accessible reasoning of the consultant is a frequently overlooked component in the consultation relationship. It is at this point that the novice can get trapped into equating consultee-centered consultation with collaboration so that reflection of this type will help. Also, Sandoval's point that the consultant should challenge his or her own theory and basically not be an ideologue, or mask his or her own priorities and feelings, is important for the consultant to monitor. Otherwise, rather than helping to move discussions along in this manner, consultee resistance is erroneously deducted and the consultant then strives to make the medicine go down, (i.e., influence the consultee to adopt the consultant's recommendations). Sandoval's article expresses the values and goals of the consultee-centered model most clearly. Thus, the prospect is increased that the professional can make clear choices of whether he or she can use this model effectively, if it is appropriate for a particular consultation situation, or if he or she is comfortable with the model from a theoretical consideration.

The next four articles capitalize on the power of a constructivist framework for the study of the consultation process. Such a paradigm leads to theory development and, as in these articles, can produce provocative ideas, which then challenge both practitioners and researchers to validate. Furthermore, the authors of these articles are clear in describing their approach and identifying the factors that need to be considered before applying their findings. Case studies are one of the obvious tools to use in studying the individual consultation approach.

Hylander's (this issue) work presents a novel way to study the conceptual shifts that the consultee, in particular, must experience in order to advance in the consultation process. The use of grounded theory to generate the concept of *turnings* will be helpful to consultants-in-training and practitioners alike. Equally important are the discoveries that the consultant must be ready to change his or her own representation of the problem, and possess the awareness and skill to utilize various models of available interactions to influence the process. This idea of *shifting* helps explain the consultation process and alleviate the dissonance that the novice often feels, which can lead him or her to the overwhelming decision to shift among models of consultation throughout the process. The thoughtful and careful use of qualitative methodology to study process opens new doors for researchers to learn more about the rough spots that are likely to occur during consultation. Hylander points the way for other qualitative researchers to advance our knowledge base. Finally, Hylander's work is most noteworthy in that it is based in part on the consultations of 23 experienced consultants, a rarity in the literature wherein the use of students-in-training as the consultant, a common necessity, is often the norm. The power of this data source is obvious since the question of the contribution of the novice's naiveté to the observations becomes a nonfactor in this study. While some earlier work (Pryzwansky, 1989) suggested that the use of experienced consultants also might not totally guarantee different results since a surprising range in problem-solving skill may still exist among expert consultants. Nonetheless, those findings do not distract from the uniqueness of the Hylander findings.

In the Webster, Knotek, Babinski, Rogers, and Barnett (this issue) article, the consultants are graduate students who are themselves receiving consultation regarding their consulting practices as part of a university project. While little is presented regarding the students' background and training, there exists the unusual element of the novice interaction, in this case with a consultee who is also new to his or her profession of teaching. The application of consultation to new teachers is an area pupil personnel service professionals, such as school psychologists, have not taken advantage of extensively. In addition to providing support and service to a potentially receptive group of consultees, this venue offers the secondary benefit of promoting closer work relationships in the future (Pryzwansky, 1996). Thus, the exciting possibilities that are inherent in this project hopefully will result in permutations of examples in the literature originating from the field. Of even greater or equal import is that this article reinforces the consideration of an overlooked strategy for the internally based consultant—that of group consultation. The possibilities are limitless for the types of groups that could be formed (e.g., teachers, parents, other support service personnel), the topics, time (e.g., limited vs. open-ended), and nature of the group (e.g., volunteer-based groups, inservice). While consultation is promoted as a service that can improve the effectiveness of the individual consultee and thus, impact more client students over time than a direct service model, the value of a group-centered approach holds even greater promise wherein efficiency concerns are touted. There are many naturally occurring groups in organizations such as the schools, so that the issue of time for consultation does not have to be a significant barrier. Schools, in particular, remain consultation and collaboration alien environments, whether an individual or group format is considered. Practitioners would be advised to explore the naturally occurring group to offer indirect service on their own or with other support service personnel.

Specifically, the skill of questioning, with the intent of going beyond a clarification, is critical to the consultant's success. Consequently, the attention directed to this skill in the Webster et. al. (this issue) article reminds us of the impact of questioning on the overall process and also provides direction the narrative can take to achieve a variety of objectives.

The opportunity to examine the work of experienced consultants and consultees wherein the goal is to facilitate change in the consultee is presented in the article by Knotek, Rosenfield, Gravois and Babinski (this issue). In addition, administrator support was high within a context of positive expectations (a new school). A collaboration process stressing problem-solving was qualitatively studied by the authors who found three traits that were especially important to Instructional Consultation (IC). Interesting, in spite of what appears as rather optimal conditions for consulting to occur, it is clear how formidable a reframing exercise can be even for an experienced consultee possessing a change orientation. Consequently, these shared observations of positive change are not to be taken lightly and point to the areas consultants need to address with all types of consultees. Also, in this instance, a rather clear but challenging prescriptive goal involved shifting the teacher's emphasis from student-orientated problems to an optimal instructional match. An instructional consultation team provided support for the consultant case managers. The team was also available to the case manager consultant–teacher consultee dyad upon request. Another intriguing aspect of IC was the range in professional identity of the case managers, suggesting that preservice training or supervision experiences were limited or nonexistent prior to the project. This observation suggests the utility of this approach for professionals from a variety of backgrounds.

Finally, the presentation by Ingraham (this issue) should be invaluable to trainers of consultants, either at the preservice or inservice levels, when multicultural matters are present. The description of the development and analysis of case studies is quite specific and comprehensive when a cultural hypothesis needs to be considered by the consultant and consultee. This investigation provides the details necessary for future development of the examination or practice elements that make up the awareness and strategic thinking of both parties to the consultation process. Ingraham is appropriately cautious regarding her conclusions in that the experiences of three second-year graduate students in her consultation course form the basis of these findings. While calling for future research, these findings should be seized upon by trainers to illustrate the patterns of interactions that students are likely to encounter when dealing with multicultural content.

This special issue presents a long-overdue contemporary discussion of the important conceptual points regarding consultee-centered consultation as well as case study research involving this model. The premise of consultee-centered consultation and the values inherent in this approach should differentiate it clearly from both other consultation models and collaboration, and in doing so advance the specificity of future research protocols. Similarly, the use of case study research by the authors in this issue illustrates the power of this investigatory tool, and at the same time provides a boost to research conducted on this consultation model. The promise of consultation as a service delivery tool in the schools has been caught up in the euphoria often associated with the many fads this system has experienced. Consultation and certainly the term collaboration have not been immune from this phenomenon and as such run the risk of becoming less popular before positive results can be demonstrated. Ironically, these approaches show no signs of diminishing in popularity among educators in spite of a lack of any semblance of a clear-cut understanding of what it means for the participants. While other professionals (e.g., architects) seem to use the term collaboration to implement specific practices, educators are still less specific. Consequently, special issues like the current one are a welcomed stimulus for the educational and psychological areas of consultation practice.

REFERENCES

Caplan, G. (1970). *The theory and practice of mental health consultation*. New York: Basic Books.

Pryzwansky, W. B. (1989) School consultation: Some considerations from a cognitive psychology perspective. *Professional School Psychology, 4,* 1-14.

Pryzwansky, W. B. (1996). Making psychologists indispensable in schools: Collaborative training approaches involving educators and school psychologists. In R. C. Talley, T. Kubiszn, M. Brassard, & R. J. Short (Eds.), *Making psychologists in schools indispensable: Critical questions and emerging perspectives* (pp 67-70). Washington, DC: American Psychological Association.

Walter B. Pryzwansky is a Professor in the School Psychology Program at the University of North Carolina at Chapel Hill and past president of the American Board of School Psychology. His professional and research interests include consultation in schools and ethics in psychology. He is the co-author, along with D. Brown and A. Schulte, of the text *Psychological Consultation* (5th ed.).

JOURNAL OF EDUCATIONAL AND PSYCHOLOGICAL CONSULTATION, 14(3&4), 369–385

THE CONSULTANT'S CORNER

Terrorism, Terrorism Threat, and the School Consultant

Judith L. Alpert and Heather Duckworth Smith
New York University

Interventions for responding to terrorism and terrorism threat are described for 2 types of preventive interventions (primary and secondary) and for 3 levels (community, school and classroom). All the interventions aim to prevent mental illness and to promote mental health. This article is based on research and literature focused on: (a) responses to human-made and natural disasters, (b) psychological resilience, and (c) programs for dealing with acute and chronic stress and anxiety. While the focus of this article is on responding to terrorism and terrorism threat, it can be generalized to other human-made or natural disasters that impact a school.

I looked up at the TV in the room and noticed debris was beginning to fall rapidly from the upper floors. I looked out the window and saw the thousands of people on the street screaming and running northward and ambulances and fire engines below the building begin to be engulfed in a pile of debris and ash. I was motionless as I realized the cloud was moving towards the school and the lights flickered and the building shook.... (Deutsch, 2001, p. 4)

NOTE: Margaret R. Rogers of the University of Rhode Island is column editor for THE CONSULTANT'S CORNER.

Correspondence should be addressed to Judith L. Alpert, Department of Applied Psychology, Steinhardt School of Education, New York University, 239 Greene Street, 5th Floor, New York, NY 10003. E-mail: judie.alpert@nyu.edu

This statement was written by a high school senior who attended one of four schools within a mile of the World Trade Center (WTC). It relates his individual experience on September 11, 2001. Some children and adults in these four schools witnessed the planes hitting the Twin Towers, people jumping from the Towers, and buildings falling. They smelled burning flesh. They saw dust-covered and terrorized people screaming and running. In addition, as the media repeatedly exposed the horrific occurrence, the atrocity was witnessed not only by those within a mile of the WTC but also by school children, school staff, parents, and others throughout the country and afar.

Presently, our nation is living with the threat of further terrorism. School staff need to prepare for the possibility of future atrocities. In addition, school staff must help individuals learn to live in these times of terrorist threat. Resilience must be fostered. Coping skills must be taught. School consultants, whether internal or external to the school, can play an important role in helping children, parents, and school staff deal with terrorism and the threat of terrorism.

In this article, interventions for responding to terrorism and terrorist threat are described for two types of preventive interventions (primary and secondary) and for three levels (community, school, and classroom). All the interventions aim to prevent mental illness and to promote mental health. Given space limitations and because tertiary prevention is usually offered outside the school system, it will not be considered here. However, it is important to note that tertiary prevention is sometimes a necessary intervention during times of terrorism and trauma.

This article is based on research and literature focused on: (a) responses to human-made and natural disasters, (b) psychological resilience, and (c) programs for dealing with acute and chronic stress and anxiety. The information about interventions is supplemented as well as informed by the experiences of Alpert and Smith and their colleagues at the time of the September 11, 2001 atrocity in New York City, Washington, DC, and Pennsylvania, its aftermath, and by research on terrorism in other locales. While the focus of this article is on responding to terrorism and terrorist threat, it may also be generalized to other human-made (e.g., school violence) or natural (e.g., hurricane) disasters that impact a school.

PRIMARY PREVENTION: INTERVENTION PRIOR TO A TERRORIST EVENT

Primary prevention has a long history of widespread support in the mental health field (Albee & Gullotta, 1997; Alpert, 1985, 1995; Alpert & Meyers, 1983). It refers to lowering the rate of new cases of mental disorders by counteracting the harmful circumstances that may produce the illness (Caplan, 1964). While it may be difficult or impossible for school consultants to prevent traumatic events, they can prepare children and adults to deal with the threat of the events as well as the events when they occur. Primary prevention involves increasing individual strengths and decreasing individual limitations as well as increasing social supports and decreasing social stresses.

Community Level: Working With Parents

At the community level, primary prevention involves preparedness and resilience training. Well before a terrorist event, parents can be prepared to respond to the psychological aspects of terrorism. A model for such a response is provided by Vernberg and Vogel (1993). Prior to a terrorist event, parents can be educated around such issues as coping with terrorism, ways of talking to children about terrorist acts, and control of media viewing. They can also be informed about common child and adolescent reactions to trauma, risk factors that may result in a more severe response, and indicators of posttraumatic stress disorder (PTSD; Williams, Zinner & Ellis, 1999).

Resilience training is an important part of primary prevention as well. While there are many definitions of resilience, Doll and Lyon (1998, p. 348) identify a central notion: Resilience "concerns successfully coping with or overcoming risk and adversity or the development of competence in the face of severe stress and hardship." School consultants may work with parents in an effort to build mentally healthy and resilient children. They can offer lectures and workshops or lead parent discussions focused on raising mentally healthy and resilient children. According to Ayalon (Ayalon & Waters, 2002), the family influence has the most profound impact on a child's ability to cope with terrorist threat. Parents must be supported in order to provide a buffer against trauma and hope in their children.

School Level: Working With School Staff

At the school level, primary prevention involves preparing a crisis plan and organizing a crisis team. The school consultant can work with other school personnel to organize a crisis team and is an important member of the team. A crisis plan is an action plan for a crisis event such as terrorism. Such a plan helps to establish a sense of control and serves to reduce anxiety. Since September 11, 2001, the U.S. Department of Education has recognized the need for schools to prepare for and respond to disasters. Through their consultation with international government officials, the Department suggests that schools conduct disaster drills, develop safety plans to address alternative forms of communication with parents in case of emergency, and provide alternate transportation for large-scale crises (Henry, 2002). In addition, the crisis team should focus on plans that improve physical safety. Research suggests that reducing physical danger may increase perceptions of control and, therefore, decrease anxiety (Vernberg & Vogel, 1993). The school facility should be inspected for safety (Nader & Pynoos, 1993) and crisis plans should be made on the basis of knowledge of the physical plant. (For more detailed information about creating crisis teams and plans, see Brock, Lazarus, & Jimerson, 2002.)

Although it is important to address physical safety, a crisis plan must also address mental health concerns. Members of the crisis team need knowledge about common child, adolescent, and adult reactions to trauma. The school consultant can develop a plan for the provision of immediate, early, and long-term mental health assistance (Nader & Pynoos, 1993). This plan should include the development of a network of school consultants with knowledge of post-disaster intervention (Vernberg & Vogel, 1993; Yule, 1998). These professionals may need to be accessed as an external crisis team to provide services to students, faculty, or parents during or after a traumatic event (Peterson, 2001). Also, they may serve as support for the school consultants who may be traumatized themselves.

Classroom Level: Working in the Classroom

School consultants can help children cope in these difficult times of war, terrorism, and terrorist threat. A focus of primary prevention with children and youth is on building their resiliency. Resilience can be taught and the focus of such an effort includes, for example, strengthening sense of self, building competence, helping the development of social supports, and assisting in development of skills including communication, conflict resolution, and peer mediation. Stress management techniques and other coping skills need to be fostered as well (Bell, 2001; Vernberg & Vogel, 1993). To build resilience in children, school consultants must be proactive in providing programs that foster resilience and in working with teachers who will be implementing or assisting in the implementation of these programs.

The available research indicates that resilience can be fostered through well-designed programs (Cowen, Wyman, Work, & Iker, 1995; La Greca & Gurwitch, 2002; Weissberg & Elias, 1993). School consultants have the knowledge and skills to design, develop, and implement such programs that focus on building resilience. There are many such programs already developed. In a report on the status of the research and research-based programs on resilience, Davis (1999) reviews the resilience literature relating to children and adolescents as well as the literature on research-based programs that foster resilience. The programs considered include programs that target families, early childhood, kindergarten, elementary, middle, and high school. Unfortunately, there is little rigorous research on these programs.

One example is the Community Oriented Preventive Education (C.O.P.E.) method for stress management (Ayalon, 1992) and for developing coping skills, which has been implemented in the entire school system in Israel. According to Ayalon (Ayalon & Waters, 2002), it has been translated into several languages and used in times of war and terrorism in the former Yugoslavia and Northern Ireland. Ayalon also utilizes a flexible and comprehensive teaching and therapeutic model (BASIC-Ph) to enhance coping skills in Israeli children. She indicates that each letter represents one type of coping that they identify and enhance through specific activities. The letters and their representation signifiers follow: B (belief), A (affect–feeling and emotions), S (social coping channel), I (imagination), C (cognitive channel), and Ph (physical coping).

In the United States, one school that offers expanded school-based mental health programs to the entire school population reported that school consultants were prepared to advise teachers and administrators about helpful school responses and classroom activities after the terrorist activities of September 11, 2001 (Harrison, 2002). They were already providing information to students and leading class discussion on such topics as stress, anger, depression and suicide. Since these school consultants had already established credibility with school administrators, teachers and students, they were able to provide early intervention and treatment following September 11, 2001.

SECONDARY PREVENTION: INTERVENTION FOLLOWING A TERRORIST EVENT

Following a traumatic event, secondary prevention is necessary to respond to the crisis and to intervene on a short-term basis. The focus is on lessening the rate of community disability by reducing the number of new disorders and shortening the duration of old ones (Caplan, 1964). There are three primary goals in responding to trauma: (a) prevention of an already chaotic situation from escalating, (b) minimization of short-term effects on those affected by the crisis, and (c) minimization of potential long-term effects on those affected by the crisis (American Academy of Experts in Traumatic Stress, 1999). Secondary prevention can enable the community to process thoughts and feelings related to the disaster.

Community Level: Working With Parents

School consultants can help parents deal with their own feelings and those of their children. If parents are not able to deal with the traumatic stress, their anxiety may negatively impact on their children. Thus, the school consultant should help parents deal with the traumatic experience before they attempt to help their child (Nader & Pynoos, 1993). Specifically, parents need help expressing their own experience and feelings as well as advice about how to talk to their children about the event.

School consultants should be prepared to have ongoing contact with parents, both formally and informally, to provide information and obtain feedback about posttraumatic reactions. Parents can be helped to talk to their children about the traumatic event. They can be educated about ways to talk to children at various ages. Younger children, for example, may require more concrete repetitions, clarifications, and metaphoric explorations of the event. Older children may benefit more from direct exploration of the events and information about common reactions (Vernberg & Vogel, 1993).

In addition, parents need information about developmentally appropriate responses to trauma (Sitterle & Gurwitch, 1999). Typical child post-traumatic reactions include fear, anxiety, re-experiencing the event, avoidance of the event and its triggers, and hyperarousal, all of which may result in dependency, regression, or reenactments. These typical reactions, in general, decrease over time. If these reactions persist for over three months, the individual is at risk for continued problems and should seek mental health services (Foa, n.d.; for a more detailed account of common and disordered child and adolescent reactions to trauma, see Appendices A and B, respectively).

School consultants can also provide parents with information about posttraumatic reactions. Individual responses to traumatic events vary based on existing factors prior to, during, and after the trauma. For example, reactions are impacted by the individual's experience of the event, relationships with those directly and indirectly affected, past history, culture, beliefs, temperament, personality (Nader, 2001), and community connectivity (Zinner & Williams, 1999; for a more detailed account of risk factors for PTSD, see Appendix C).

Based on what is known about children's responses to traumatic events and resilience, La Greca and Gurwitch (2002) maintain that children need to be provided with information about the event and about typical reactions to traumatic events to help normalize feelings, their social supports need to be enhanced, and their coping strategies developed. School consultants can elicit parent help in this process. La Greca, Sevin, and Sevin (2001) have developed *Helping America Cope*, a parent–child workbook designed to help children cope with terrorist attacks. In addition, an anniversary edition has been completed that has an additional focus on preparedness (La Greca & Gurwitch, 2002).

Following a terrorist event, parents should be encouraged to send their children to school. Children who resume their regular activities and roles as children may benefit from social support and structure (Vernberg & Vogel, 1993). Parents should monitor their child's media exposure (Perry, n.d.-b). For example, studies indicate a relationship between television viewing of the Oklahoma City bombing and reported degree of distress (Pfefferbaum et al., 2001). Parents should be informed that children are likely to do better when parents openly discuss events, concerns, and feelings (Nader & Pynoos, 1993).

School Level: Working With School Staff

At the school level, the school consultant should be prepared to consult with the administration, faculty, and other mental health professionals during the crisis phase. School leaders had to respond immediately to the September 11, 2001, terrorist activity. For example, school administrators in the vicinity of the WTC had to decide whether it was safer to remain in the building or evacuate (Deutsch, 2001). Even schools further away from the WTC had to make difficult decisions including whether to close, whether to arrange transportation for those who lived far from school and, whether and how much to disclose to the students. Important decisions need to be made immediately following a disaster. Making decisions following a disaster is difficult as it is a time when there is often high emotional and physical arousal, uncertainty, and fear. Anticipating some possible events and responses prior to a terrorist event may be helpful at the time of a terrorist event. School consultants can assist in decision-making.

During the initial impact of a disaster, school consultants should provide psychological first aid. They can provide support for leaders and help-providers, gather and give age-appropriate information, reunite families, notify individuals of deaths and injuries, and conduct initial interviews with those who witnessed the event. This initial contact with aftected groups and individuals, however, should not be in the form of critical incident stress debriefing (CISD). That is, recent research does not support encouraging people to express their feelings or providing them with information about the event or advice about behaviors to engage in following the disaster (Foa, n.d.; Ruzek & Watson, 2001; van Emmerik, Kamphuis, Hulsbosch, & Emmelkamp, 2002). The research has shown that these brief, one-session interventions shortly after the trauma do not have a positive impact on mental health. Moreover, CISD may impede the natural recovery process, as it may inadvertently cause victims to bypass the support of family and friends (van Emmerik, et al. 2002). While Vernberg and Vogel (1993) note that establishing early contact with affected individuals increases the chances that assistance will be accepted at a later time, the more recent research indicates that early contact should serve to assess one's immediate safety, reduce anxiety, and prevent disorientation (Yule, 1998). In addition, people should be reunited with family as soon as possible.

During times of crisis teachers should have the opportunity to both participate in groups and have individual consultations with the school consultant. Topics addressed may concern, for example, how student behavior and school performance may change, when to refer a child for mental health services, and how to adapt class pace and content for students' developmental age and level of trauma experienced. Teachers should recognize that their students might be overwhelmed, confused, sad, and fearful after a traumatic event. Students may regress and there may be more behavioral and emotional problems resulting in less learning capabilities. These responses are generally short-term and, with reassurance, patience, and nurturing, usually resolve (Perry, n.d.-a). Teachers should set reasonable limits on behavior. Reducing stress is also beneficial to students after a traumatic event (Nader, 2001). For example, after September 11, one high school near the WTC temporarily suspended homework and school activities, and promoted students spending more time with family and friends (Vizzini, 2001).

Teachers need consultation regarding how to be helpful to students. Also, teachers need to be supported themselves during and after the time of trauma. They, too, may be traumatized. For example, faculty and staff may need some free periods in the aftermath of a trauma or they may need relief from other duties. It must be recognized that the tasks of faculty and staff following a traumatic event may be more burdensome, numerous, and stressful due to the traumatic event. For example, there may be an increase in paperwork or an increase in students visiting the nurse with somatic complaints (Nader & Pynoos, 1993). At the same time, it is important for faculty and staff to recognize that their actions have an effect on students. While it is important that no one be pushed to express feelings, it is also important to remember that children and adolescents often mirror the responses of adults (Perry, n.d.-a).

In our experience, after September 11, 2001, teachers in some schools were more traumatized than the students. Some schools responded to the teachers' needs. One school enabled teachers to meet informally with school consultants. The same school organized monthly teacher-appreciation days. Special events (i.e., a jazz performance) for faculty and staff were arranged after school dismissal. Such events enabled the faculty to have time to talk to each other and to relate common experiences and feelings.

Although there is little research about the positive effects of memorials, rituals, and anniversary ceremonies, they are believed to serve important psychological functions. They are symbolic communal responses (Zinner & Williams, 1999), public expressions of grief and support, remembrances of victims, and a review and interpretation of the disaster. They provide closure and help people cope with bereavement (La Greca, 2001; Vernberg & Vogel, 1993). Symbolic ceremonies can enable the positive re-direction of emotions associated with trauma and bring people together (Sitterle & Gurwitch, 1999).

School consultants can work with students and school staff to plan memorials, rituals, and ceremonies. School consultants, for example, helped to organize some of the following events on the first anniversary of September 11, 2001: a memorial ceremony, classroom activities that involved writing letters to grieving families, and the creation of a public space where students could relate thoughts and feelings.

Most important, however, the first step in being able to help others is to be psychologically stable oneself (Nader, 2001; Poland & McCormick, 1999). Thus, consultants should consult with other mental health professionals to meet their own mental health needs. Issues of confidentiality may impede the school consultant's ability to fully benefit from the survivor group. Therefore, it may be beneficial for school consultants in different settings to sustain each other. School consultants should follow the recovery advice that they give to their clients (Poland & McCormick, 1999).

Classroom Level: Working in the Classroom

In the aftermath of trauma, children and adolescents need social support from family members, teachers, peers, and people in similar circumstances (general supportive behaviors) and coping assistance (actions taken by parents, teachers, or friends that help people cope with stressful events;

Prinstein, La Greca, Vernberg, & Silverman, 1996). While elementary school students report that parents and friends offer more coping assistance than teachers (La Greca, 2001), the potential influence that teachers and other school staff can have on children's recovery should not be discounted (Prinstein et al.). For example, teachers, assisted by school consultants, can help students process the event through discussions, reenactment activities, or games; they can foster an environment in which students return to their normal roles and routines. Children also can be active in a symbolic way or by helping others in some altruistic act. In this way, they become empowered (Ayalon & Waters, 2002).

One excellent resource for both teachers and school consultants is the Internet. In the wake of September 11, 2001, the web sites by the American Psychological Association (http://helping.apa.org), the National Association of School Psychologists (NASP; http://www.nasponline.org), and the International Society for Traumatic Stress Studies (http://istss.org) had a plethora of information about common reactions to trauma and PTSD, as well as suggestions for how to assist the school community. In addition, there are several trauma treatment manuals that have been developed in response to both September 11 and other natural or human-made disasters that may be useful in guiding disaster-related discussion and activities (Gurwitch & Messenbaugh, 2001; La Greca, Sevin, & Sevin, 2001).

School-based interventions should take place in the classroom, as it is a familiar setting that may promote a sense of community (Vernberg & Vogel, 1993). The school consultant and teacher can help students deal with stressors and ongoing problems resulting from the tragedy. They should also work to reduce stress and promote positive coping methods (La Greca, 2001). Thus, secondary prevention incorporates primary prevention in that students are aided in recovery from the initial disaster while also prepared to cope with any future traumatic events.

Students need to be provided with factual information that is developmentally appropriate; a sense of safety and control; and assistance in identifying, labeling, and expressing emotions as well as in normalizing routines and roles (La Greca, 2001; Vernberg & Vogel, 1993). The child's lead should be followed, and short discussions rather than one long talk is often most helpful. Misperceptions should be clarified, and questions should be answered (Perry, n.d.-b). For example, children and adolescents may have some of the following concerns: Are we safe? Is my town next? Will there be another attack? Could this happen to us? Why was mom crying? What will happen to me if my parents die? How can I help? Why do I have to go to school? Who is responsible? What will be done about it? Why did this happen? (American Psychological Association, 2001; Nader, 2001; NASP, 2001). School consultants and teachers should be prepared to address such concerns. The responses should be honest and reassuring. The main message to communicate is that local and national leaders are working to make their environment as safe as possible. Disaster-related projects can supplement and facilitate discussions.

Throughout the early intervention phase, children who are in need of additional services must be identified (La Greca, 2001). People who seem more upset immediately, who have more devastating losses (e.g., death of a parent), or who present with more severe symptomatology after 1 month are those who should be watched carefully. In schools, parents, teachers, and school consultants can work together to target such individuals who may need to be referred for mental health services outside of school.

CONCLUSION: RESPONSIBILITIES FOR TRAINERS AND SCHOOL CONSULTANTS

There is an important role for school consultants in schools in these times of terrorist activity and threat. School consultants have contact with parents, school administrators, faculty, and students. They can reach many people. School consultants know how to plan interventions and to develop programs based on need. They can educate others about mental health issues (Alpert, 1985).

School consultants can engage in primary prevention activity by conducting preparedness activities and resilience training. They can work to prepare the school community to deal with traumatic events. They can take actions to prevent long-term mental health problems for parents, school staff, and students. Important activities include educating the school community about common reactions to trauma, creating an environment for discussion and expression of feelings, and engaging in activities that continue to build resilience in the population. Should symptomatology persist after a disaster, school consultants have the skills to recognize symptomatology and to treat individuals or to make mental health referrals.

These are difficult times. They point to responsibilities for university trainers and for practicing school consultants. Universities must assume responsibility for training school consultants to respond in these troubled times, and school consultants, who have not had such training, must attain it.

REFERENCES

Albee, G. W. & Gullotta, T. P. (1997). Primary prevention's evolution. In G. W. Albee & T. P. Gullotta (Eds.), *Primary prevention works* (pp. 3–22). Thousand Oaks, CA: Sage.

Alpert, J. L. (1985). Change within a profession: Change, future, prevention, and school psychology. *American Psychologist, 40,* 1112–1121.

Alpert, J. L. (1995). *Psychological consultation in educational settings.* Northvale, NJ: Aronson.

Alpert, J. L., & Meyers, J. (1983). *Training in consultation: Perspectives from mental health, behavioral, and organizational consultation.* Springfield, IL: Thomas.

American Academy of Experts in Traumatic Stress. (1999). *A practical guide for crisis response in our schools* (4th ed.). Commack, NY: Author.

American Psychiatric Association. (1994). *Diagnostic and statistical manual of mental disorders* (4th ed.). Washington, DC: Author.

American Psychological Association. (2001, September 12). *A forum discussion guide for APA members: Talking with youth about traumatic events.* Retrieved February 6, 2002, from http://www.apa.org/practice/ ptforum.html

Ayalon, O. (1992). *Rescue! Community oriented preventive education handbook: Helping children cope with stress.* Ellicott City, MD: Chevron Publishing.

Ayalon, O., & Waters, F. S. (2002). The impact of terrorism on Jewish Israel: An interview with Ofra Ayalon. *Journal of Trauma Practice, 3 & 4,* 133–154.

Bell, C. C. (2001, November). Cultivating resiliency in youth. *Journal of Adolescent Health, 29,* 375–381.

Brock, S. E., Lazarus, P. J., & Jimerson, S. R. (2002). *Best practices in school crisis prevention and intervention.* Bethesda, MD: NASP Publications.

Caplan, G. (1964). *Principles of preventive psychiatry.* New York: Basic Books.

Cowen, E.L., Wyman, P.A., Work, W.C., & Iker, M.R. (1995). A preventive intervention for enhancing resilience among highly stressed urban children. *Journal of Primary Prevention, 15,* 247–260.

Davis, N. J. (1999). *Resilience: Status of the research and research-based programs.* Manuscript in progress.

Deutsch, A. (2001, Fall). An administration in crisis. *The Spectator: The Stuyvesant High School Newspaper,* pp. 4–5.

Doll, B., & Lyon, M. A. (1998). Risk and resilience: Implications for the delivery of educational and mental health services in the schools. *School Psychology Review, 27,* 348–363.

Foa, E. B. (n.d.). *Guidelines for response to the tragic events in the U.S.* Retrieved February 6, 2002, from http://www.istss.org/terrorism/Guidelines%20for%20Response.pdf

Gurwitch, R. H., & Messenbaugh, A. K. (2001). *Healing after trauma skills.* Oklahoma City, OK: University of Oklahoma Health Sciences Center.

Gurwitch, R. H., Silovsky, J. F., Schultz, S., Kees, M., & Burlingame, S. (n.d.). *Reactions and guidelines for children following trauma/disaster.* Retrieved September 16, 2001, from http://www.apa.org/practice/ptguidelines.html

Harrison, M. M. (2002, Spring). Comprehensive coverage. *Teaching Tolerance,* 49–56.

Henry, T. (2002, February 18). Schools may do terror-evacuation drills: Officials hope to borrow U.S. military lessons. *USA Today,* p. 12B.

La Greca, A. M. (2001). Children experiencing disasters: Prevention and intervention. In J. Hughes, A. M. La Greca, & J. C. Conoley (Eds.), *Handbook of psychological services for children and adolescents* (pp. 195–222). Oxford, England: Oxford University Press.

La Greca, A. M., & Gurwitch, R. (2002, August). *Resilience in children exposed to (disasters and) terrorism: Putting "science" into "practice."* Paper presented at the meeting of the American Psychological Association on Psychology Responds to Terrorism, Chicago, IL.

La Greca, A. M., Sevin, S. W., & Sevin, E. L. (2001). *Helping America cope.* Coral Gables, FL: 7-Dippity, Inc.

La Greca, A. M., Silverman, W. K., Vernberg, E. M., & Roberts, M. C. (2002). *Helping children cope with disasters and terrorism.* Washington, DC: American Psychological Association.

Lahad, S., Shacham, Y., & Niv, S. (2000). Coping and community resources in children facing disaster. In A. Y. Shalev, R. Yehuda, & A. C. McFarlane (Eds.), *International handbook of human response to trauma* (pp. 389–395). New York: Kluwer Academic.

Nader, K. (2001). *Terrorism: September 11, 2001 trauma, grief, and recovery.* Retrieved February 6, 2002, from http://www.sourcemaine.com/gift/html/firstaid.html

Nader, K., & Pynoos, R. (1993). School disaster: Planning and initial interventions. *Journal of Social Behavior and Personality*, 8. Retrieved February 6, 2002, from http://www. Sourcemaine.com/gift/Html/nader.html

National Association of School Psychologists. (2001, November). *Children and fear of war and terrorism: Tips for parents and teachers.* [Brochure]. Bethesda, MD: Author.

Perry, B. D. (n.d.-a). *Children and loss.* Retrieved February 6, 2002, from http://teacher.scholastic.com/professional/bruceperry/childrenloss.htm

Perry, B. D. (n.d.-b). *Coping with traumatic events: terrorist attacks in the United States.* Retrieved February 6, 2002, from http://www.childtrauma.org/Traumatic_ events_teachers.htm

Peterson, J. (2001, September 12). *Talking with children about traumatic events.* Retrieved September 16, 2001, from http://www.apa.org/practice/ptmemo.html

Pfefferbaum, B., Nixon, S., Tivis, R., Doughty, D., Pynoos, R., Gurwitch, R. H., & Foy, D. (2001). Television exposure in children after a terrorist incident. *Psychiatry, 64,* 202–211.

Poland, S,. & McCormick, J. S. (1999). Who cares for the caregiver? In S. Poland & J. S. McCormick (Eds.), *Coping with crisis* (pp. 317–326). Longmont, CO: Sopris West.

Prinstein, M., La Greca, A. M., Vernberg, E. M., & Silverman, W. K. (1996). Children's coping assistance: How parents, teachers, and friends help children cope after a natural disaster. *Journal of Clinical Child Psychology, 25,* 463–475.

Ruzek, J., & Watson, P. (2001, Fall). Early intervention to prevent PTSD and other trauma-related problems. *PTSD Research Quarterly*, 12(4), 1–3.

Sitterle, K. A., & Gurwitch, R. H. (1999). The terrorist bombing in Oklahoma City. In E. S. Zinner & M. B. Williams (Eds.), *When a community weeps: Case studies of group survivorship* (pp. 160–189). Ann Arbor, MI: Taylor & Francis.

van Emmerik, A. A. P., Kamphuis, J. H., Hulsbosch, A. M., & Emmelkamp, P. M. G. (2002). Single session debriefing after psychological trauma: A meta-analysis. *The Lancet, 360,* 766–771.

Vernberg, E., & Vogel, J. (1993). Part 2: Interventions with children after disasters. *Journal of Clinical Child Psychology, 22,* 485–498.

Vizzini, D. (2001, Fall). 'Normal' redefined for students. *The Spectator: The Stuyvescent High School Newspaper,* p. 21.

Vogel, J., & Vernberg, E. (1993). Part 1: Children's psychological responses to disasters. *Journal of Clinical Child Psychology, 22,* 464–484.

Weissberg, R. P., & Elias, M. J. (1993, Fall). Enhancing young people's social competence and health behavior: An important challenge for educators, scientists, policymakers, and funders. *Applied & Preventive Psychology, 2,* 179–190.

Williams, M. B., Zinner, E. S., & Ellis, R. R. (1999). The connection between grief and trauma: An overview. In E. S. Zinner & M. B. Williams (Eds.), *When a community weeps: Case studies of group survivorship* (pp. 3–17). Ann Arbor, MI: Taylor & Francis.

Yule, W. (1998). Posttraumatic stress disorder in children and its treatment. In T. W. Miller (Ed.), *Children of trauma: Stressful life events and their effects on children and adolescents* (pp. 219–243). Madison, CT: International Universities Press, Inc.

Zinner, E. S., & Williams, M. B. (1999). Summary and incorporation: A reference frame for community recovery and restoration. In E. S. Zinner & M. B. Williams (Eds.), *When a community weeps: Case studies in group survivorship* (pp. 237–254). Ann Arbor, MI: Taylor & Francis.

APPENDIX A
COMMON CHILD AND ADOLESCENT REACTIONS
TO TRAUMA

Whether an individual is affected directly or indirectly, traumatic events have an impact. The severity of and exposure to the stressor influences the degree of one's reactions (Vogel & Vernberg, 1993). Even unexposed children may develop posttraumatic stress reactions (Nader & Pynoos, 1993). The length of reactions varies depending on the cause of the stressor. After natural disasters, posttraumatic symptoms can last up to 3 years, although they tend to abate by 9 months. However, reactions to human made disasters may persist longer (Vogel & Vernberg). Reports by teachers indicate that there is classroom disruption for over a month following a disaster (Nader & Pynoos).

Reactions to trauma are developmentally bound. Some possible reactions based on grade level include the following (Gurwitch, Silovsky, Schultz, Kees, & Burlingame, n.d.):

Kindergarten and Elementary School

(a) Anxiety, fear, or worry about safety of self and others, which may result in more clingy behavior; (b) worry about the re-occurrence of violence; (c) distress which may result in irritability or moodiness; (d) behavior changes such as increased activity level, decreased concentration or attention, withdrawal, angry outbursts, aggression, or absenteeism; (e) increased somatic complaints; (f) changes in school performance; (g) recreating events through conversation or play; (h) increased sensitivity to sounds associated with the trauma; (i) statements and questions about death; (j) changes in sleep or appetite; (k) lack of interest in usual activities; (l) increased negative behaviors or emotions; (m) regression in behaviors; and (n) statements of hate or anger.

Middle School

(a) Feelings of anxiety, worry, and fear about safety of self and others; (b) worries about the re-occurrence of terrorism or the consequences of war; (c) changes in behavior, such as decreased attention or concentration, increased hyperactivity, changes in academic performance, irritability, anger outbursts or aggression; (d) withdrawal, or absenteeism; (e) somatic complaints; (f) discomfort with feelings, especially those associated with revenge; (g) increased likeliness of discussing gruesome details; (h) repeated discussion of the event; (i) increased sensitivity to sounds associated with the trauma; (j) lack of trust in and negative perception of others, particularly those that are different; (k) repetitive thoughts and comments about death and dying; (l) changes in sleep or appetite; (m) lack of interest in usual activities; (n) increased negative behaviors or emotions; (o) statements of hate or anger; and (p) denial of impact of events.

High School

(a) Worry, fear, and anxiety about safety of self and others; (b) worries about the re-occurrence and repercussions of event; (c) changes in behavior, such as withdrawal, irritability, anger outbursts or aggression, academic performance, attention or concentration, hyperactivity, absenteeism; (d) discomfort with feelings especially those of revenge and vulnerability; (e) increased risk of substance abuse; (f) discussion of events and reviewing details; (g) less trust in and negative perception of others, especially those that are different; (h) increased sensitivity to sounds associated with the trauma; (i) repetitive thoughts and comments about death and dying, including suicidal ideation; (j) changes in sleep or appetite; (k) lack of interest in usual activities; (l) increased negative behaviors or emotions; (m) statements of hate or anger; and (n) denial of impact of events.

APPENDIX B
DISORDERED CHILD AND ADOLESCENT
REACTIONS TO TRAUMA

Generally, reactions to traumatic events are temporary, but it is possible for the symptoms to persist. Three months after Hurricane Andrew one-third of the students reported severe to very severe levels of PTSD symptomatology, and at 7 months, this statistic had only dropped to 18% (Prinstein et al., 1996). Likewise, 5 to 15 months after the Chowchilla bus kidnapping, 73% of the 23 child-victims interviewed had moderate to severe symptoms of PTSD (Vogel & Vernberg, 1993). Therefore, it is necessary for mental health personnel, faculty, and parents to be cognizant of the boundaries between normal reactions to stressful events and more severe symptoms. Of note are several more possible paths to disordered reactions to trauma, including (a) concerns about safety and security that may manifest in attachment problems, (b) decreased attention and concentration that may lead to academic decline, and (c) withdrawal and negative views of others and/or the future that may result in depression. There are also other reactions that may develop into phobias, anxiety disorders, or even PTSD (La Greca, 2001). However, most children are resilient (La Greca, 2001; Vogel & Vernberg, 1993).

If disturbed behavior following a traumatic event persists for longer than 1 month, the person is at greater risk of having or developing PTSD. As described by the *Diagnostic and Statistical Manual of Mental Disorders* (American Psychiatric Association, 1994), PTSD is characterized by reexperiencing phenomena (e.g., recurrent thoughts or dreams), avoidance of stimuli, numbing of emotional reactions, and hyperarousal (e.g., difficulty sleeping or concentrating) to the point that it causes significant distress or impairment in functioning. In children, the features of the disorder may manifest in reenactment play, frightening dreams, or disorganized, agitated behavior.

APPENDIX C
RISK FACTORS FOR PTSD

Reactions to trauma are impacted by the individual's experience of the event, relationships with those directly and indirectly affected, past history, culture, beliefs, biochemical and physiological makeup, temperament, personality (Nader, 2001), and community connectivity (Zinner & Williams, 1999). The two factors that have the greatest impact on posttraumatic reactions are: (a) the severity of personal exposure to traumatic event (Sitterle & Gurwitch, 1999; Zinner & Williams), and (b) the extent to which loved ones are affected (Sitterle & Gurwitch; Vogel & Vernberg, 1993). There is conflicting research about which is more predictive. Based on research after the Oklahoma City bombing, Sitterle and Gurwitch (1999) found the strongest predictor of PTSD to be direct exposure to the life threatening events. In contrast, Lahad, Shacham, and Niv (2000), and Vogel and Vernberg (1993), based on research after a fatal school bus–train collision, assert that the number of people one mourns is more important than proximity to the event.

Other factors leading to more severe posttraumatic reactions include the duration of the event, malicious intent, and one's level of defenselessness (American Psychological Association, 2001; Zinner & Williams, 1999). Damage resulting in dislocation to home increases immediate distress but does not have long-term affects (Vogel & Vernberg, 1993). Life experience also matters. Children who have experienced more traumas, have mental health problems, and have experienced violence in the home in early child-hood are more at risk for developing PTSD, for example (La Greca, Silverman, Vernberg, & Roberts, 2002).

Certain variables are more age-specific. Child reactions are more acute if parents are involved in the emergency effort, the military, or the reserves (NASP, 2001). In addition, children have stronger reactions when they are separated from their parents during the stressful events (Vogel & Vernberg, 1993) or during evacuation (Lahad et al., 2000). Most adoles-cents grasp the meaning of death. Some seek out friends at these times. Others withdraw. Those with a history of depression, suicidal behavior, and chemical dependency are at risk for prolonged and serious reactions (NASP, 2001). Similarly, adults who experience guilt and increased re-sponsibility have a greater chance of developing more traumatic responses (Nader & Pynoos, 1993).

Judith L. Alpert is Professor of Applied Psychology at New York University. She teaches a 2-semester school consultation practicum course and a course on trauma and has written exten-sively in both areas. She supervises psychologists and psychologists-in-training around trauma as well as provides direct service to those involved in traumatic events.

Heather Duckworth Smith is a graduate student and Graduate Student Worker at New York University. She supervises school psychology students who consult in schools and has worked in schools around September 11th and its aftermath.

Please submit manuscripts and address inquiries regarding The Consultant's Corner column to Margaret R. Rogers, PhD; Psychology Department; Uni-versity of Rhode Island; Chafee 419; Kingston, RI 02881; 401-874-7999; mrogres@uri.edu; Fax: 401-874-2157.

JOURNAL OF EDUCATIONAL AND PSYCHOLOGICAL CONSULTATION, 14(3&4), 387–399

DIVERSITY IN CONSULTATION

Teaching on Racism: Tools for Consultant Training

Jason J. Washburn
Northwestern University Feinberg School of Medicine

Theodoric Manley, Jr. and Frank Holiwski
DePaul University

Diversity is becoming an increasingly important consideration in the consultation field. Consultants are often in a unique position to make significant individual and organizational change with respect to diversity. As the field beings to develop cross-cultural consultation competencies and skills, it is important to emphasize the sociopolitical factors of diversity, specifically oppression. Lessons learned from a course on White racism are presented, with a focus on strategies for identifying and changing contemporary racist behavior. These lessons are presented as useful foundations for training preservice or inservice consultants to address diversity concerns and related systems of oppression.

Educational and psychological consultants are increasingly faced with diversity concerns in school, mental health, workplace, and sports-related

NOTE: Mary M. Clare of Lewis & Clark College is column editor for DIVERSITY IN CONSULTATION.

Correspondence should be addressed to Jason J. Washburn, 710 N. Lake Shore Drive, Suite 900, Chicago, IL 60611–3078. E-mail: j-washburn@northwestern.edu

settings (Butryn, 2002; Ingraham & Meyers, 2000; Ivancevich & Gilbert, 2000; Trickett, Barone, & Watts, 2000). Although the demand for culturally competent consultation is likely to continue to increase, research has only begun to examine the impact of cultural factors on the delivery of consultation services (Rogers, 2000). Additionally, opportunities for formal education and ongoing training in culturally competent consultation have generally been limited (Steward, 1996). Considering that culturally competent consultation will likely improve the effectiveness of consultation services (Tarver Behring & Ingraham, 1998), it seems important for graduate training and continuing education programs to provide increasing opportunities for the development of cross-cultural consultation skills.

Several cross-cultural consultation competencies were recently identified in a mini-series devoted to diversity and school-based consultation in *School Psychology Review* (Ingraham & Meyers, 2000). Culturally competent consultation skills may include culturally appropriate communication and interpersonal skills, an understanding of the cultural context of consultation, and the acquisition of culture-specific knowledge (Rogers, 2000). The development of cultural competence for consultation also requires an understanding of the sociopolitical factors associated with diverse groups. As Green (1998) succinctly writes, "Cultural, racial, and sexual orientation differences are *not* problems in and of themselves. Prejudice, discrimination, and other forms of aggressive intercultural conflict based on those differences *are* problems," (p. 100). As such, the development of culturally competent consultation skills must also embrace critical multicultural and race theories (e.g., Delgado, Stefancic, & Harris, 2001; Kinlochoe & Steinberg, 1997) to fully understand and attend to the oppression of diverse groups.

Consultants are often in the unique position of having influence over the systemic factors that perpetuate prejudice, discrimination, and intercultural conflict. Specifically, they have the training, skills, and privileges to examine and intervene at multiple levels within a system or institution. Consequently, consultants can maximize the impact of their diversity interventions by not only addressing individual-level thoughts, feelings, and behaviors, but also by working within systems to address organizational-level policies and procedures (Plummer, 1998).Addressing diversity and oppression at the individual and organizational levels requires an examination of diversity *isms*. By diversity isms, we refer to attribute nouns (Saucier, 2000) that represent social attitudes and beliefs related to diverse groups, such as racism, sexism, heterosexism, ageism, classism, and ableism. Examining diversity isms is a formidable task that is often met with significant resistance and conflict (Karp & Sammour, 2000;

Schmitz, Stakeman, & Sisneros, 2001). Addressing diversity isms, particularly with members from dominant groups (i.e., White, male, heterosexual, economically stable), can sometimes result in divisiveness, hostility, and backlash (Hemphill & Haines, 1997). Accordingly, training consultants for increased culturally competence must include a specific focus on historical and contemporary systems of oppression, as well as the tools for addressing individual and organizational manifestations of the diversity isms.

MANAGING, MOTIVATING, AND CHANGING:
A PEDAGOGICAL INTERVENTION FOR RACISM

Since 1998, we have worked with more than 500 students and community members in a course titled "White Studies and Eradicating White Racism." The course, which was created and developed by the second author and members of the Hoop Institute[1], was conceptualized as an action research pedagogy with the specific purpose of bringing students, particularly members of the dominant racial group, out of a denial status regarding racial issues and into one that is aware, conscientious and ideologically, emotionally, and behaviorally congruent. The course content focused on several concepts specifically related to racism in the United States, including the historical and social construction of the White and Whiteness, White privilege, the invisibility of White, and the historical and contemporary impact of White racism on White and nonwhite groups.

The participants in the course have primarily included upper-class undergraduate and graduate students who elected to take the course for college credit. The course has also been offered as a workshop and provided to public school teachers, members of community organizations, and other adult community members. Members of both the dominant and the non-dominant racial groups enrolled in the course, including those of African (13%), Asian (12%), European (58%), and Latino–Latina (9%) descent.

Many lessons were learned during the more than five years of conducting, modifying, and evaluating this course. Three lessons appear applicable to the cross-cultural training of consultants, particularly with regard to addressing inculturated bias systems or diversity isms. Specifically, we have learned to place an increasingly strong emphasis on contemporary forms of racism, to directly address denial of continued racism in the

---

[1] The Hoop Institute (www.hoopinstitute.org) is a non-profit service and educational organization committed to improving the lives of working disenfranchised communities.

United States, and to provide guidance and strategies for changing contemporary racism.

"I AM NOT A RACIST!"

Perhaps the most significant lesson we have learned during the evolution of the course has been the need for increasing our emphasis on contemporary versus traditional forms of racism (Wells, 1998). Contemporary racism has been variably labeled in the literature as *aversive racism* (Gaertner & Dovidio, 1986), *subtle* or *symbolic racism* (Sears, 1988), or *modern racism* (McConahay, 1986). In contrast to traditional racism, contemporary racism embraces egalitarian and nonprejudicial beliefs, attitudes, and values, while continuing to engage in racial discrimination (Gaertner & Dovidio). Rather than clearly prejudicial behaviors or attitudes, contemporary racism presents through subtle and indirect forms, often outside an individual's awareness (Banaji & Dasgupta, 1998). Research suggests that contemporary racists often rationalize or justify their behavior on information that supports common stereotypes, rather than basing their behavior directly on an individual's racial category (Brief, Dietz, Cohen, Pugh, & Vaslow, 2000; Gaertner & Dovidio, 1986). Contemporary racists are especially likely to engage in discriminatory behavior when social norms are ambiguous (Hodson, Dovidio, & Gaertner, 2002).

Examples of contemporary forms of racism are abundant. For example, while contemporary racists are unlikely to discriminate against a strong job applicant solely on the basis of race, they are more likely to make racially discriminatory decisions if the applicant has mixed credentials (Hodson et al., 2002). Contemporary racism can also be found in political support for positions that deny the existence of racism or oppose strategies to address inequality, such as affirmative action programs. For example, Sawires and Peacock (2000) demonstrated that contemporary racist beliefs (i.e., minorities are accessing more than their share of resources) were positively related to support for California's Proposition 209, which prohibits the consideration of race, sex, color, ethnicity, or national origin in decisions related to public employment, education, or contracting. Contemporary racism can also be found in the portrayal of African American and Latino or Latina criminal suspects as more threatening than White suspects on television news programs (Chiricos & Eschholz, 2002).

Understanding contemporary racism is critical in training consultants about diversity and culturally competent practice, since most trainees are unlikely to publicly endorse traditionally racist beliefs or attitudes (Devine & Elliot, 2000). Indeed, our quantitative and qualitative research findings have clearly demonstrated that the majority of our students endorse an ideology of equality and egalitarianism. While our students embrace such ideologies, these ways of thinking may be in conflict with their feelings, automatic thoughts, and behaviors, particularly among members of the dominant racial group. This kind of conflict is evident in the subscale profiles of our White students who completed the White Identity Attitude Scale (WIAS; Helms, 1990). Without exception, every class of White students has reported a strikingly similar pattern of subscale scores on the WIAS. Specifically, the students that consistently reported a greater endorsement of racial humanism (Autonomy scale) and recognition of the sociopolitical implications of race (Pseudo-Independence scale), also gave less endorsement to racial confusion and self-disorientation (Disintegration scale) and to active or passive racial superiority (Reintegration scale). While this pattern suggests an ideology that supports equality and egalitarianism, our White students also reported mid-range endorsement of racial naiveté and lack of racial awareness (Contact scale), a finding that is not theoretically consistent with racial humanism (Hardiman, 1982).

Additional measures, checklists, and our White students' journal entries also indicated a conflict between an egalitarian ideology and nonegalitarian thoughts, feelings, and behaviors (e.g., feeling uncomfortable in a group of non-Whites, participating in racially derogatory jokes and conversations). We came to the conclusion, as suggested by others (i.e., Krysan, 1998), that the greater endorsement of the Autonomy and Pseudo-Independence subscales reflected a socially desirable and egalitarian ideology, and not necessarily a unified set of egalitarian or racially humanistic thoughts, feelings, or behaviors.

As consultants in cultural competence trainings are also likely to present with egalitarian ideologies and anti-racist intentions, focusing on traditional forms of racist beliefs and behaviors is unlikely to be productive. Instead, we have found it useful to address contemporary forms of racism directly, particularly with members of the dominant racial group. However, solely providing information about contemporary racism has had little affect due to our students' difficulty in applying this knowledge to their personal experience. For example, our White students often enacted the finger-pointing strategy, in which they acknowledged that *other* people perpetrated contemporary racism, but denied that they engaged in such behavior. Consequently, we found it necessary to specifically demonstrate the ways in which our students personally and specifically participate in contemporary forms of racism. We suggest that similar demonstrations will assist consultants in becoming increasingly self-reflective and disclosing with regards to diversity concerns.

"RACISM IS OVER!"

Before contemporary racism can be identified or addressed in consultant trainees, it is necessary to examine if consultants endorse the common belief that systemic racism no longer exists in the United States (Crosby, Bromley, & Saxe, 1980; Dovidio, Gaertner, Kawakami, & Hodson, 2002; Stephan & Stephan, 1999). We found that our White students were more likely to believe that, except for limited problems with traditionally racist groups (i.e., the Ku Klux Klan), the civil rights movement has accomplished its goal and the races are generally equal. This belief system worked well in reducing cognitive dissonance for many of our White students who were, thereby, able to profess an ideology of equality that was consistent with their perception that the United States is generally free of racism.

Several strategies can be employed to provide evidence for the continued existence of racism. While research findings from the social science literature can be useful (e.g., Delgado & Stefancic, 1997; Feagin, Vera, & Batur, 2001; López, 1996), scholarly evidence alone is likely to be insufficient. As with contemporary forms of racism, it has been necessary for us to personalize the research so that our students can directly apply these data to their daily lives. To accomplish this goal, we have used a variety of checklists, exercises, and essays to delineate and quantify how contemporary and traditional forms of racism continue to affect the personal lives of our students (e.g., White Benefits Checklist, Kivel, 1996; Demographic Power Analysis, Hoop Institute, 1998). We have also found it vital to strategically clarify definitions of racism. Considering the extreme defensive reaction associated with being labeled a racist, we found it best to emphasize the link between institutional power and racism, thereby de-emphasizing the labeling of individuals as racists. By differentiating systematic racism from individual-level stereotypes, prejudices, and discrimination, our students became less defensive and more open to acknowledging and expressing their true thoughts, feelings, and behaviors. In addition, we were able to address accusations of reverse-racism by clarifying that any member of any racial group can be discriminatory, while only members of the dominant racial group have the collective institutional and sociopolitical power to perpetuate and benefit from systematic racism.

Once our students became more aware of the continued existence of systematic racism, it was possible to demonstrate how they personally engaged in contemporary forms of racism. Several methods and measures are available for demonstrating contemporary racism. One of the most powerful procedures currently available is the Implicit Attitudes Test (Greenwald, McGhee, & Schwartz, 1998). This computer-based test identifies unconscious racial biases through a paired-association task. We also presented the subscale profile of the WIAS and discussed the theoretical incongruence between the endorsement of both racial naiveté and racial humanism. In addition, we introduced the possibility of social desirability by presenting data demonstrating that our experimental Social Desirability for Racism scale (Manley & Washburn, 2000) accounts for a significant proportion of variability in the Autonomy and Pseudo-Independence subscales of the WIAS (Manley, Washburn, & Holiwski, 2002).

An effective method for eliciting conflicting feelings and automatic thoughts has been to require our students to write in journals after each class. This has been a powerful tool for bypassing the cognitive "politically correct" censor that often impedes classroom discussions. It has also been useful to present autobiographical accounts of racist thoughts, feelings, and behaviors (i.e., Clark & O'Donnell, 1999). By "spilling the beans," members of the dominant racial group assist in establishing a norm for disclosing the secrets of contemporary racism (Clark, 1999). Finally, we continuously identified and discussed incidents in which our students engaged in contemporary forms of racism in the classroom.

The receptivity of consultant trainees to acknowledgement and examination of their own participation in contemporary forms of racism can be facilitated by several additional approaches. Taking a cue from Linehan's (1993) Dialectical Behavior Therapy, we have found it important to challenge our students' denial and defensiveness while also validating their feelings of dissonance and desire for egalitarianism. We believe it is important to highlight that most members of the dominant racial group have egalitarian and anti-racist intentions and ideologies, even when they engage in or experience racist thoughts, feelings, or behaviors. We have also found it useful to mitigate our students' dissonance to avoid the reactionary responses that are common in the Reintegration process (Helms, 1990). We do this by contextualizing contemporary racism within normative racial socialization practices in the United States, thereby providing a frame for our students to disengage from self-blame (e.g., "I'm a bad person if I have racist thoughts"). This process has freed our students, particularly among members of the dominant racial group, to more openly acknowledge, express, and evaluate their feelings, automatic thoughts, and behaviors.

"WELL, WHAT CAN I DO ABOUT IT?"

We have found the dissonance created with the conflict between students' ideologies and racist feelings, automatic thoughts, and behaviors typically motivate them to action. It was common for our students, particularly members of the dominant racial group, to begin searching for immediate solutions at the first sign of dissonance. These immediate solutions often consisted of nominal approaches to the problems of racism, such as sending money to anti-racist or multicultural organizations. Members of the dominant racial group also tended to focus on how to help the victims of racism through paternalistic strategies, such as assisting with the assimilation of members of diverse groups into the dominant culture. While many students sought quick fixes, some students expressed interest in making dramatic changes in their lives. For instance, some embraced the New Abolitionist's strategy of attempting to renounce the privileges associated with being White (Ignatiev, 1997), while others made significant life changes, such as moving to a diverse neighborhood or changing their career.

We believe it is important to encourage consultants in cultural competence trainings to struggle with the dissonance rather than making immediate life changes or attempting to help members of non-dominant groups. The initial insight and understanding that motivates one to action is likely insufficient for making significant and meaningful change. We have found it necessary for our students to develop a more in-depth and personal understanding of the complexities of human diversity and systems of racism before moving to action. We are especially concerned that social action without a deeper level of understanding and personal insight may lead to greater harm than good. For example, the primary author, a White male, rose to a leadership position shortly after he joined a feminist organization during his undergraduate education. Since he was not sufficiently aware of his sexist thoughts, feelings, and behaviors, he exercised a dominant and controlling style over the organization, alienating some members and perpetuating sexist roles. Using this example in the classroom, we have emphasized the real possibility that good intentions without sufficient personal awareness and knowledge can often lead to negative outcomes.

Instead of rushing to change themselves or others, we encourage our students to begin by understanding how they participate in contemporary forms of racism. To facilitate this process, we provide practical strategies for gaining increasing awareness of racist thoughts, feelings, and behaviors (i.e., thought records). We have found it useful to present an onion analogy for the awareness process. Specifically, we suggest that a thick outer layer of political correctness and social desirability often covers racist thoughts, feelings, and behaviors. Once the outer layer is removed, each layer of racist thoughts, feelings, and behaviors that becomes exposed and acknowledged leads to increased awareness of other, often more pungent layers of racist thoughts, feelings, and behaviors.

With increased awareness of contemporary forms of racism, our students become ready to challenge and change their thoughts, feelings, and behaviors. Before discussing ways to change contemporary racism, we present popular strategies that have proven ineffective in the psychological and educational literature, such as the "I have a Black friend" strategy, a simplistic variation of the Contact Hypothesis (Allport, 1954; Pettigrew & Tropp, 2000). We also provide specific cognitive and behavioral strategies for altering contemporary forms of racism, such as cognitive retraining exercises (Devine & Monteith, 1993; Stangor, Thompson, & Ford, 1998). We teach our students to deliberately identify and evaluate the contributions of their racist thoughts, feelings, and behaviors to their everyday decisions and choices. We also encourage our students to consciously consider how the outcomes of their decisions and choices either perpetuate or challenge racism. Students from dominant and nondominant racial groups have also found it useful to explore their own racial or ethnic identity using existing identity development models (e.g., Hardiman, 1982; Helms, 1990). Finally, we encourage our students to continue to participate in this process with other motivated members of their racial group and to seek out environments that are intolerant of traditional and contemporary forms of racism.

Because diversity training programs often fail to transfer skills to everyday life (Hemphill & Haines, 1997), we require our students to integrate the course lectures, readings, discussions, exercises, in-class research, and other materials into a social action paper. The social action paper assists students in defining a personal goal and requires them to delineate specific steps to reach that goal at both individual and ecological levels[2]. The final result of the social action paper is not only a demonstration of students' competency with the course material, but also a specific and detailed plan for individual and social change.

---

[2]We do not evaluate students on the basis of their ideology or force students to change their ideology. Instead, we encourage students to focus on goals that increase the congruence between their ideologies and their thoughts, feelings, and behaviors, even if their ideologies are not egalitarian or anti-racist.

CONCLUSION

We have found the strategies and approaches used in our course to be useful for addressing contemporary forms of racism in adult students and community members (Manley, Washburn, & Holiwski, in press). Similar strategies and approaches may be useful in cultural competency trainings for consultants. Further research is needed to examine the applicability and effectiveness of these procedures for developing cultural competencies with consultants. It is likely that our techniques will need to be modified and adapted to the specific contexts in which consultants practice, such as educational systems, mental health facilities, and organizations. Further research is also necessary to explore longitudinal outcomes of cultural competency trainings. Although raising awareness of contemporary racism is an important and vital step in the training of consultants, the ultimate goal is a tangible change in consultation practice towards greater cultural competence.

Although our work has focused specifically on racism, we believe the lessons learned during the evolution of this course are also applicable to other types of diversity isms and concerns. It is important to acknowledge that racism, sexism, classism, heterosexism, and other forms of diversity isms dynamically interact to influence the consultation process. It is our hope that these and other strategies can assist in the training of consultants to more effectively address multiple and interacting forms of oppression. By educating, motivating, and equipping future consultants with the tools for increased social awareness and social change, we believe consultation can play an invaluable role in addressing social injustices.

REFERENCES

Allport, G. W. (1954). *The nature of prejudice.* Cambridge, MA: Addison-Wesley.

Banaji, M. R. & Dasgupta, N. (1998). The consciousness of social beliefs: A program of research on stereotyping and prejudice. In V. Y. Yzerbyt, G. Lories & B. Dardenne (Eds.), *Metacognition: Cognitive and social dimensions* (pp. 157–170). London: Sage.

Brief, A. P., Dietz, J., Cohen, R. R., Pugh, S. D., & Vaslow, J. B. (2000). Just doing business: Modern racism and obedience to authority as explanations for employment discrimination. *Organizational Behavior and Human Decision Processes, 81,* 72–97.

Butryn, T. M. (2002). Critically examining White racial identity and privilege in sport psychology consulting. *Sport Psychologist, 16,* 316–336.

Chiricos, T., & Eschholz, S. (2002). The racial and ethnic typification of crime and the criminal typification of race and ethnicity in local television news. *Journal of Research in Crime and Delinquency, 39,* 400–420.

Clark, C. (1999). The secret: White lies are never little. In C. Clark & J. O'Donnell (Eds.), *Becoming and unbecoming White: Owning and disowning a racial identity. Critical Studies in Education and Culture Series* (pp. 92–100). Westport, CT: Bergin & Garvey.

Clark, C., & O'Donnell, J. (Eds.). (1999). *Becoming and unbecoming White: Owning and disowning a racial identity.* Westport, CT: Bergin & Garvey.

Crosby, F., Bromley, S., & Saxe, L. (1980). Recent unobtrusive studies of Black and White discrimination and prejudice: A literature review. *Psychological Bulletin, 87*, 546–563.

Delgado R., & Stefancic, J. (1997). *White studies: Looking behind the mirror.* Philadelphia: Temple University Press.

Delgado, R., Stefancic J., & Harris, A. (2001). *Critical race theory: An introduction.* New York: New York University Press.

Devine, P. G., & Elliot, A. J. (2000). Are racial stereotypes really fading? The Princeton trilogy revisited. In C. Stangor (Ed.), *Stereotypes and prejudice: Essential readings. Key readings in social psychology* (pp. 86–99). Philadelphia: Taylor & Francis.

Devine, P., & Monteith, M. (1993). The role of discrepancy-associated affect in prejudice reduction. In D. Mackie & D. Hamilton (Eds.), *Affect, cognition and stereotyping: Interactive processes in group perception* (pp. 317–344). San Diego, CA: Academic.

Dovidio, J. F., Gaertner, S. E., Kawakami, K., & Hodson, G. (2002). Why can't we just get along? Interpersonal biases and interracial distrust. *Cultural Diversity & Ethnic Minority Psychology, 8*, 88–102.

Feagin, J. R., Vera, H., & Batur, P. (2001). *White racism: The basics* (2nd ed.). New York: Routledge.

Gaertner, S. L., & Dovidio, J. F. (1986). The aversive form of racism. In J. F. Dovidio & S. L. Gaertner (Eds.), *Prejudice, discrimination, and racism* (pp. 61–89). San Diego, CA: Academic.

Green, R. J. (1998). Race and the field of family therapy. In M. McGoldrick (Ed.), *Re-visioning family therapy: Race, culture, and gender in clinical practice* (pp. 93–110). New York. Guilford.

Greenwald, A. G., McGhee, D. E., & Schwartz, J.L.K. (1998). Measuring individual differences in implicit cognition: The implicit association test. *Journal of Personality and Social Psychology, 74*, 1464–1480.

Hardiman, R. (1982). White identity development: A process oriented model for describing the racial consciousness of White Americans. *Dissertation Abstracts International, 43*, 104.

Helms, J. E. (1990). *Black and White racial identity: Theory, research, and practice.* Westport, CT: Greenwood.

Hemphill, H., & Haines, R. (1997). *Discrimination, harassment, and the failure of diversity training: What to do now.* Westport, CT: Quorum Books.

Hodson, G., Dovidio, J. F., & Gaertner, S. L. (2002). Processes in racial discrimination: Differential weighting of conflicting information. *Personality and Social Psychology Bulletin, 28*, 460–471.

Hoop Institute. (1998). *Demographic power analysis.* Unpublished manuscript. Chicago: Author.

Ignatiev, N. (1997). *The point is not to interpret Whiteness but to abolish it.* Paper presented at the 1997 Conference on the Making and Unmaking of Whiteness. Retrieved May 20, 2003 from http://racetraitor.org/abolishthepoint.pdf

Ingraham, C. L., & Meyers, J. (2000). Introduction to multicultural and cross-cultural consultation in schools: Cultural diversity issues in school consultation. *School Psychology Review, 29*, 315–19.

Ivancevich, J. M., & Gilbert, J. A. (2000). Diversity management: Time for a new approach. *Public Personnel Management, 29*, 75–92.

Karp, H. B., & Sammour, H. Y. (2000). Workforce diversity: Choices in diversity training programs and dealing with resistance to diversity. *College Student Journal, 34*, 451–458.

Kinlochoe, J., & Steinberg, S. (1997). *Changing multiculturalism*. Buckingham, England: Open University Press.

Kivel, P. (1996). *Uprooting racism: How White people can work for racial justice*. Philadelphia: New Society Publishers.

Krysan, M. (1998). Privacy and the expression of White racial attitudes: A comparison across three contexts. *Public Opinion Quarterly, 62*, 506–544.

Linehan, M. M. (1993). *Cognitive-behavioral treatment of borderline personality disorder*. New York: Guilford.

López, I.F.H. (1996). *White by law: The legal construction of race*. New York: New York University Press.

Manley, T., & Washburn, J. J. (2000). *A measure of social desirability for racial identity and attitudes scales*. Unpublished manuscript, DePaul University, Chicago.

Manley, T., Washburn, J. J., & Holiwski, F. (2002). *Social Desirability Scale data and White racial attitude measures*. Unpublished raw data.

Manley, T., Washburn, J. J., & Holiwski, F. (in press). Teaching about White racism in the United States: Does it make a difference? In T. Fong (Ed.), *Handbook of research methods in ethnic studies*. Walnut Creek, CA: Altamira Press.

McConahay, J. B. (1986). Modern racism, ambivalence, and the Modern Racism Scale. In J. F. Dovidio & S. L. Gaertner (Eds.), *Prejudice, discrimination, and racism* (pp. 91–125). San Diego, CA: Academic.

Pettigrew, T. F., & Tropp, L. R. (2000). Does intergroup contact reduce prejudice: Recent meta- analytic findings. In S. Oskamp (Ed.), *Reducing prejudice and discrimination. The Claremont symposium on applied social psychology* (pp. 93–114). Mahwah, NJ: Lawrence Erlbaum Associates, Inc.

Plummer, D. L. (1998). Approaching diversity training in the year 2000. *Consulting Psychology Journal: Practice & Research, 50*, 181–189.

Rogers, M. R. (2000). Examining the cultural context of consultation. *School Psychology Review, 29*, 414–418.

Saucier, G. (2000). Isms and the structure of social attitudes. *Journal of Personality & Social Psychology, 78*, 366–385.

Sawires, J. N., & Peacock, M. J. (2000). Symbolic racism and voting behavior on Proposition 209. *Journal of Applied Social Psychology, 30*, 2092–2099.

Schmitz, C. L., Stakeman, C., & Sisneros, J. (2001). Educating professionals for practice in a multicultural society: Understanding oppression and valuing diversity. *Families in Society, 82*, 612–622.

Sears, D. O. (1988). Symbolic racism. In P. A. Katz & D. A. Taylor (Eds.), *Eliminating racism: Profiles in controversy. Perspectives in social psychology* (pp. 53–84). New York: Plenum.

Stangor, C., Thompson, E., & Ford, T. (1998). An inhibited model of stereotype inhibition. In R. Wyer (Ed.), *Advances in social cognition* (pp. 193–210). Mahwah, NJ: Lawrence Erlbaum Associates, Inc..

Stephan, W. G., & Stephan, C. W. (1999). An integrated threat theory to prejudice. In S. Oskamp (Ed.), *Reducing prejudice and discrimination* (pp. 23–45). Mahwah, NJ: Lawrence Erlbaum Associates, Inc.

Steward, R. J. (1996). Training consulting psychologists to be sensitive to multicultural issues in organizational consultation. *Consulting Psychology Journal: Practice and Research, 48*, 180–189.

Tarver Behring, S., & Ingraham, C. L. (1998). Culture as a central component of consultation: A call to the field. *Journal of Educational and Psychological Consultation, 9*, 57–72.

Trickett, E. J., Barone, C., & Watts, R. (2000). Contextual influences in mental health consulta-
tion: Toward an ecological perspective on radiating change. In J. Rappaport & E. Seidman
(Eds.), *Handbook of community psychology* (pp. 303–330). Dordrecht, Netherlands: Kluwer
Academic.
Wells, L. (1998). Consulting to Black–White relations in predominantly White organizations.
Journal of Applied Behavioral Science, 34, 392–396.

Jason J. Washburn is completing a postdoctoral fellowship in clinical child psychology at the
University of Michigan Medical School. He will soon be joining the Psycho-Legal Studies program at Northwestern University as a Northwestern Juvenile Project research scholar. His interests are in juvenile delinquency, racism, and clinical child psychology.

Theodoric Manley, Jr. is an Associate Professor of sociology at DePaul University and CEO of
the Hoop Institute. Dr. Manley teaches on race and ethnic relations from a community perspective. He is former director of DePaul's Center for African American research.

Frank Holiwski is a graduate student and part-time instructor in the Department of Psychology at DePaul University. Mr. Holiwski's interests are in White racism and community psychology.

Please submit manuscripts and address inquiries regarding the Diversity in
Consultation column to Mary M. Clare, Ph.D.; MSC 86, Counseling Psychology; Lewis & Clark College; Portland, OR 97219; 503-768-6069;
henning@lclark.edu; Fax: 503-768-6065.

JOURNAL OF EDUCATIONAL AND PSYCHOLOGICAL CONSULTATION, *14*(3&4), 401–403

 # BOOK AND MATERIAL REVIEWS

Child Abuse and Neglect: The School's Response, by Connie Burrows Horton and Tracy K. Cruise, New York: Guilford, 2001, 204 pp.

Review by
Jerry L. Kernes
California State University, Long Beach

Children who commit violent acts are often themselves victims of severe abuse and neglect (Salzinger, 1999). Although it is true that not all children who suffer maltreatment become aggressive, evidence suggests that abuse and aggression are not separate phenomena (Dwyer, Osher, & Warger, 1998). Since the recent tragic events at Columbine and Santee, schools throughout the nation have been asked to prevent future violence and identify children at risk for committing such acts. In *Child Abuse and Neglect: The School's Response*, Connie Burrows Horton and Tracy K. Cruise attempt to answer that call by providing a comprehensive analysis of child maltreatment.

The authors skillfully integrate findings from recent child maltreatment literature and link them to practical applications in school-based settings. Hypothetical case examples are used throughout the text to illustrate research findings and humanize theoretical concepts.

The first chapter provides an overview of child maltreatment, including definitions, statistical reports of incidence and prevalence, risk factors, and

---

NOTE: This book review was accepted and prepared by Clyde Crego of California State University, former editor for the BOOK AND MATERIAL REVIEWS column.

Correspondence should be addressed to Jerry L. Kernes, Department of Psychology, California State University, Long Beach, 1250 Bellflower Boulevard, Long Beach, CA 90840–0111. E-mail: jlkernes@att.net

consequences of child abuse and neglect. The following two chapters focus on the various issues involved with the identification and reporting of child abuse and neglect. The authors carefully delineate the logistics of reporting by addressing follow-through procedures after a report of child maltreatment has been made. The remaining five chapters emphasize clinical issues of particular interest to school-based professionals. It is here that the book shines most brightly.

Chapters 4 and 5 address the ways in which the mental health and counseling needs of children can most adequately be met. Strategies and specific guidelines are provided for both referral and in-school treatment options. In addition to covering the basic details and dos and don'ts of suggested practice, the authors give consideration to the emotional experiences of all involved parties.

Chapters 6 and 7 highlight consultation with individuals in key positions in the life of the maltreated child, as well as the planning and implementation of effective victim prevention programs. The consultation chapter includes useful reproducible overhead transparency masters for use in inservice training programs focusing on definitions of child abuse and neglect, incidence and prevalence of child abuse and neglect, possible indicators of child abuse and neglect, mediators of the effects of child maltreatment, reporting abuse, making the report, and obstacles to reporting. The consultation chapter provides invaluable tools to school-based professionals, while the prevention chapter adds greater theoretical understanding to the importance of the arguments raised in the introductory chapter.

The book closes with an important chapter on identifying and preventing compassion fatigue. The authors sensitively address the emotional burdens that school professionals face in their response to child maltreatment. Warning signs of compassion fatigue are presented alongside ideas for intervention with the goal of increasing school professionals' ability to monitor and care for themselves.

Connie Burrows Horton and Tracey K. Cruise have produced a timely, relevant, and practical guide to detect, respond to, and prevent child maltreatment. Their book provides an intelligent synthesis of the most recent research literature on child maltreatment with tangible practice guidelines. *Child Abuse and Neglect: The School's Response* is a valuable resource for any school-based mental health consultant. It would also serve as an excellent text for students in a variety of academic disciplines including social work, school counseling, school psychology, human services, and education.

REFERENCES

Dwyer, K., Osher, D., & Warger, C. (1998). *Early warning, timely response: A guide to safe schools.* Washington, DC: U.S. Department of Education.

Salzinger, S. (1999). Determinants of abuse and the effects of violence on children and Adolescents. In A. J. Goreczny & M. Hersen (Eds.), *Handbook of pediatric and adolescent health psychology* (pp. 429-449). Boston: Allyn & Bacon.

Jerry L. Kernes is a lecturer in both the Psychology Department and the Educational Psychology Department at California State University, Long Beach. He teaches human sexuality at both the graduate and undergraduate level, as well as undergraduate courses in career development and psychological assessment. His research interests are in the areas of positive psychology and clinical decision making.

Prospective reviewers as well as authors who are interested in having their books and other materials reviewed should contact Emilia C. Lopez, Queens College—CUNY, Educational and Community Programs, 65-30 Kissena Blvd., Flushing, NY 11367. E-mail: lopez@cedx.com

JOURNAL OF EDUCATIONAL AND PSYCHOLOGICAL CONSULTATION, 14(3&4), 405–407

BOOK AND MATERIAL REVIEWS

Traumatic Brain Injury in Children and Adolescents: Assessment and Intervention, by Margaret Semrud-Clikeman, New York: Guilford, 2001, 211 pp.

Review by
Valerie L. Williams
VA Sierra Nevada Health Care System and
University of Nevada School of Medicine

This book is part of the Guilford School Practitioner Series and it is written to provide professionals who are not neuropsychologists with an "understanding of the underpinnings of head injury, beginning with definitions, incidence, and sequelae." The book is enjoyable to read and does a thorough job of introducing the reader to functional neuroanatomy, neuropsychological concepts, and the influence of family variables on children and adolescents who suffer brain injury. Case examples are covered in detail and skillfully integrated into the informative content of the book. Federal laws governing the definition and rehabilitation of brain injured children and adolescents are reviewed and integrated with assessment and intervention concepts. The decreased validity of commonly used measures in assessing brain injured children are openly discussed and alternative approaches clearly explained.

NOTE: This book review was accepted and prepared by Clyde Crego of California State University, former editor for the BOOK AND MATERIAL REVIEWS column.

Correspondence should be addressed to Valerie L. Williams, VA Sierra Nevada Health Care System, Mental Health Service (116B), 1000 Locust Street, Reno, NV 89502. E-mail: valerie.williams@med.va.gov

The book includes 10 chapters, beginning with an introduction that describes the presentation of a 16-year-old male who is recovering from a traumatic brain injury. Definitions of mild, moderate, and severe head injury are covered, and the demographics and medical assessment process are described. Chapters 2 and 3 present a theoretical framework for understanding the development of the central nervous system, as well as a basic description of functional neuroanatomy. The neuropsychological concepts of intellectual, academic, attentional, executive, memory, perceptual, and psychosocial functions are addressed. History of behavioral and academic disturbances that are present prior to head injury, as well as the influence of family and home–school partnerships are discussed in Chapter 4.

Chapter 5 is especially informative in providing an overview of the Individuals with Disabilities Education Act (IDEA) and Section 504 of the Rehabilitation Act of 1973 and the inclusion of traumatic brain injury as a recognized disability in 1993. An outline for gathering a developmental history is included and the relevance of three different approaches (Halstead-Reitan, Luria-Nebraska, and Boston Process Approach) to neuropsychological assessment are thoroughly explained. The author then returns to the case described in the introduction to the book, presenting test findings, diagnostic impressions, and recommendations for intervention. A second case provides an example of an evaluation conducted with a child with a premorbid history of learning difficulties and behavioral problems. One of the strengths of the book is that the author, Dr. Semrud-Clikeman, provides a clear and explicit description of a hypothesis-testing approach that has been cloaked in confusing jargon and vague generalities by other writers.

Chapters 7 through 9 may be the most useful for professionals who face the challenges of consulting and designing interventions in school settings. There are inconsistencies across states in terms of how eligibility for IDEA is defined and in what services are available for implementing Individualized Educational Plans. An outline of questions to be addressed in planning school reentry is presented and the concept of an Individualized Transition Plan for adolescents moving into adult vocational and college settings is discussed. A case study illustrating the implementation of neuropsychological recommendations is presented. Specific classroom interventions for remediating attentional, memory, and academic deficits are described in detail and pharmacotherapeutic considerations are given brief, but helpful, coverage. In Chapter 10, Dr. Semrud-Clikeman shares parting thoughts about the issues of mild head injury (not considered a disability under IDEA), family variables, therapy issues, and training issues. The brevity of this book is a welcome feature for busy professionals and it provides a useful reference to be used in daily practice. The book would also be useful as a supplemental text in graduate level assessment courses and is informative to neuropsychologists who work primarily with an adult population.

Valerie L. Williams is a psychologist at the VA Sierra Nevada Health Care System in Reno, Nevada, and Assistant Professor of Psychiatry and Behavioral Sciences at the University of Nevada School of Medicine. Her interests include behavioral medicine, neuropsychological assessment, and training in clinical psychology.

Prospective reviewers as well as authors who are interested in having their books and other materials reviewed should contact Emilia C. Lopez, Queens College-CUNY, Educational and Community Programs, 65-30 Kissena Blvd., Flushing, NY 11367. E-mail: lopez@cedx.com

JOURNAL OF EDUCATIONAL AND PSYCHOLOGICAL CONSULTATION, *14*(3&4), 409–412

Index to Volume 14
(2003)

Columns

The Consultant's Corner

Diversity in Consultation

Washburn, J. J., Manley, T., Jr., & Holiwski, F. Teaching on White Racism: Tools for Consultant Training, 387–399.

Book and Material Reviews

Kernes, J. L. [Review of *Child Abuse and Neglect: The School's Response* by C. Burrows and T. K. Cruise], 401–403.

Williams, V. L. [Review of *Traumatic Brain Injury in Children and Adolescents* by M. Semrud-Clikeman], 405–407.

Special Issues & Mini-Themes

Erchul, W. P. Special Issue: Communication and Interpersonal Processes in Consultation (Issue 2).

Knotek, S. E., & Sandoval, J. Special Issue: Consultee-Centered Consultation (Issues 3 & 4).

Other

Acknowledgments: Ad Hoc Reviewers and Editorial Board.
Article of the Year Award (2004), 241.

T - #0140 - 270225 - C0 - 229/152/10 - PB - 9780805895612 - Gloss Lamination